14

F 2017

CONTENTS

An Entry To The Log Book	4	はじめに
Local Yarn Shop	7	街の毛糸屋さん
On the Hook	9	秋のかぎ針プロジェクト
CRAFT GUIDE TO LONDON	11	ロンドン・クラフトガイド
London, Pink	25	ロンドンのピンク
The Story of GENMOU	53	GENMOU が海を渡るまで。
Through the Lens	57	レンズの向こうに
Lori's Notebook	58	Lori のプロジェクトノート
Bookish	61	ブックレビュー
Contributors	62	寄稿者紹介
Editors	63	amirisu について
Casting Off	64	後記
Patterns	66	パターン集
Credits	114	クレジット

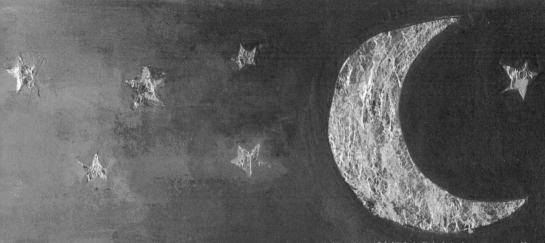

As knitters and wool lovers, the UK and its capital city London have been at the top of our dream destination list, but unfortunately, we haven't had the chance to visit since becoming knitaholics. In 2016, Tokuko and I met Allison of Yarn in the City, and when she gifted us a copy of their craft guide, the idea of a collaboration immediately popped into mind. We are thrilled that our very first collaboration on craft guides is here! We also braved asking Susan Cropper, the owner of Loop in London and a tastemaker in the global knitting community, her favorite places to visit on her weekends.

The result is a rich list of recommendations; long enough for multiple visits to the city, while also visiting museums, palaces and gardens.

Looking forward to popping on a tube with you and amirisu Issue 14 as we head to London!

Tokuko & Meri

ウールと編みものが大好きな私たちにとって、ロンドン、そしてイギリスはどうしても訪れたい場所のひとつ。でもこの仕事を始めてからまだ機会に恵まれていません。そんななか 2016 年の TNNA で、ロンドンで Yarn In The City というユニットを組んでいるアリソンと出会いました。彼女たちが出版したばかりのロンドンのクラフトショップガイドを見て、「そうだ、何か一緒にできないかな」というアイデアがすぐに浮かんだのです。その出会いから 1 年半、初めてコラボレーションによるクラフトガイドが実現してとても嬉しく思います。さらに、ロンドンの有名店 Loop のオーナーであり、世界の編みもの界を牽引していると言っても過言ではない、スーザン・クロッパーさんにお気に入りの場所を教えてもらいました。

おかげで、博物館や宮殿、公園などを観光しながらとなると、ロンドンを何度も訪れないと回りきれないほどのリストが完成しました。

私たちもこの号を片手に、ロンドンの地下鉄に乗り込みたいと思います。ロンドンで会いましょう！

トクコ＆メリ

An entry to the log book

Artwork by Maya Durham

作品提供

https://amirisu.myshopify.com/

パターン名：Arvia
デザイナー：Anna Nikipirowicz

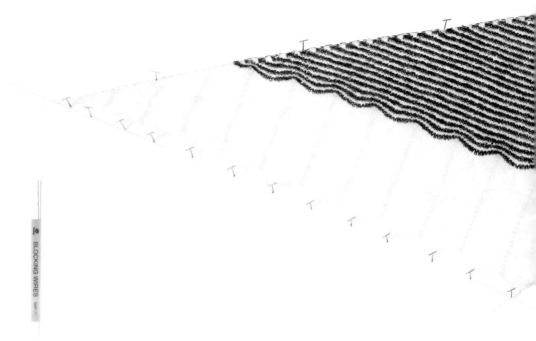

ブロッキングワイヤー

BLOCKING WIRES

編み上がった作品に ひと手間加えて、もっと綺麗に仕上げてみませんか

Take time to reach perfection.

NEW

チューリップ株式会社
〒733-0002 広島市西区楠木町 4-19-8
TEL：082-238-1144
www.tulip-japan.co.jp　info@tulip-japan.co.jp

Tulip Company Limited
4-19-8, Kusunoki-Cho, Nishi-Ku, Hiroshima
733-0002 JAPAN
www.tulip-japan.co.jp　info@tulip-japan.co.jp

オンラインショップ 全国送料無料

TULIP CRAFT CAFE　チューリップクラフトカフェ
www.tulip-japan.com

Tulip
―針は愛情―

Knit with Attitude, London

ロンドン、Knit with Attitude

When Maya first moved from Norway, where yarn shops were virtually on every street corner, to London, she was surprised that there were only a few decent yarn shops there. Encouraged by the "craftivist" movement in the early 2000s, she decided to open a yarn shop specializing in ethical and sustainable yarn - Knit with Attitude. They make a point of knowing the story behind each yarn they carry, bringing contemporary designs to customers of all generations, and overcoming the stereotypical image of knitting. Knit with Attitude shares its premises with an art gallery - the two shops complement each other beautifully and offer a unique experience to visitors.

街のいたるところに毛糸屋がある母国のノルウェーからロンドンに越してきた、オーナーのマヤ。良い毛糸ショップが少ないのに驚いたそう。材料までこだわって手作りをすることで環境問題などに貢献しようという「クラフティヴィスト」活動に刺激を受け、サステイナブルな毛糸だけを扱うお店を作ろうと決意。今でも仕入れている全ての毛糸について、誰がどんな風に作っているのかというストーリーを大事にしているとのこと。編み物の古いイメージを壊したい、というお店はアートギャラリーと空間をシェアしていて、お互いが雰囲気を高め合う素敵な場所になっています。

Address: 127 Stoke Newington High Street, N16 0PH London

Website: http://knitwithattitude.com

Choose timeless.

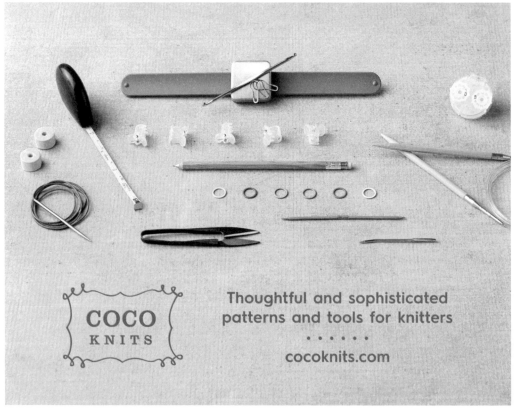

Photos courtesy of DARUMA

On the hook

秋のかぎ針プロジェクト
Designed by DARUMA

Do you like to crochet jute or raffia bags in the summer, or do you like to crochet but dislike coarse yarn? Then this bag may be the perfect fall pattern for you! Crochet in lace-weight cotton yarn. Turn to page 110.

夏はラフィアや麻紐のバッグを編むという方にも、硬い糸はちょっと苦手という方にも、この秋オススメなのがレース糸で編む小ぶりなバッグ。立体的な菱形の模様がアクセントに。 P112 参照。

WELDON ALPACA WRAP

DESIGN BY VIRGINIA SATTLER-REIMER

PATTERN NO.:	FOR USE WITH:
20175	BABY ALPACA (SPORT WEIGHT)

CRAFT CITY GUIDE TO

London

Curated by Yarn In The City

クラフト・シティ・ガイド：ロンドン
by Yarn In The City

Yarn In The City, the duo behind the book London Craft Guide and the annual event The Great London Yarn Crawl, curated this issue's Craft City Guide to London. And we have a special treat for you - Susan Cropper of Loop London is guiding you to her favorite places in town!

Photos, except otherwise noted, are by Yarn In The City

ロンドンでヤーンクロール（毛糸屋めぐりのイベント）を毎年主催し、「ロンドン・クラフトガイド」を上梓した2人組、Yarn In The City が本号のクラフトガイドのキュレーターで登場。さらに、Loop のオーナーであるスーザン・クロッパーさんのオススメの場所も紹介します！

Exploring the City...

ロンドンの街を訪ねて

By Yarn In The City

Ray Stitch - see page 22.

As outsiders, it often seems to us that everyone in London is from some place else. You can hear several languages as you travel from one point to another on the tube, and not just from tourists! London is an energetic, cosmopolitan city with a myriad of cultures and points of view, and this diversity colours everything.

Despite its size, London is anything but anonymous. Neighbourhood pockets feature local flavour and personality; London craft shops are no different. How else to explain the vibrancy and assortment of yarn, fabric and haberdashery shops that stretch across the city?

Every year when we plan the Great London Yarn Crawl, our goal is to show yarn lovers the variety of shops that London has to offer. Participants come back year after year, determined to try a route with shops that they haven't visited before

自分も含め他所からやってきたものからすると、ロンドンの誰もがロンドン出身ではないように思えます。地下鉄に乗れば一駅の間に、いくつもの言語がそこここから聞こえてきますが、見れば観光客だけでなく住んでいる人もたくさんいます。ロンドンはエネルギー溢れる、とても国際色豊かな街。様々な文化や視点が混じり合い、多様性が色々な物事をかたち作っているのです。

その大きさに反して、ロンドンはとても地元色豊かな街でもあります。それぞれの地域に地元の文化や住人の気質が感じられるのですが、手芸ショップも例外ではありません。街中に散らばる毛糸やファブリック、手芸店の多様性や個性がそれを証明しています。

毎年グレート・ロンドン・ヤーンクロール（ロンドン中の毛糸ショップを回るイベント）を行なっていますが、ロンドンにいかに多様なお店があるかを参加者に知ってもらいたいという思いで計画しています。たいていの参加者は来る年も来る年も参加しては、まだ

so that they can see them all. The GLYC focuses on 12 main shops but there are many more, and with London's population of over 8.7 million people, it's no wonder they're all different and stand apart from each other.

There are shops that specialise in British and locally-sourced yarns, others that import international and luxury yarns or focus on traditional, well-known British brands. There's a shop that carefully and ethically considers the source of the yarns they carry and shops that are true haberdasheries with fabric and notions among their wares, too.

We love that word, haberdashery. In North America it is often used in connection with shops stocking men's clothing and accessories like hats and ties. In the UK a haberdashery is a treasure chest shop of sewing notions such as buttons, zippers and thread. The Haberdashers' Livery Company, one of the Great Twelve Livery Companies, is a collection of ancient and modern trade associations and guilds in the City of London that dates back to the 14th century. Members made their living by selling small wares such as buttons and ribbons, pins, beads and other small ephemera. They were joined in the early 16th century by the hatmakers' fraternity, and afterwards there were two types of haberdashers: those of hats, and those of small wares – which is a long way round to one of the things we love most about London, and the UK: its history. From architecture to art to the cobblestones under your feet, ancient stories and inspiration abound. London is an ideal gateway to the rest of the country and its great history in textile arts: Shetland, Fair Isle, Aran, and more. And of course there are the sheep! Over 60 different breeds of sheep are found in the UK, more than any other country. As wool lovers, there's no better place to be.

Not that other fibres aren't wonderful, but we've found that wool is king in the UK. With years of history and tradition wrapped up in its cultural DNA, yarn shops are still referred to as wool shops more often than not. There is a fierce pride for British-grown and British-made products, especially wool. From podcasters like Knit British to activist movements like Wovember, and shows that champion wool and heritage such as Shetland Wool Week, the whole country is a

行ったことのないルートを巡って全店制覇するぞと意気込んでいます。GLYC は 12 店をメインに展開しつつ、それ以外にもオプションとなるお店がたくさんリストアップされているのですが、本当に様々なお店があるのもロンドンの 870 万人という人口を考えると不思議ではないのかもしれません。

国産や地元産の毛糸に特化したお店があるかと思えば、高級な輸入糸を扱うお店、またはよく知られたナショナルブランドの毛糸を売るお店もあります。そして、製造過程にこだわったサステイナブルな毛糸だけを扱うお店、そして生地や洋裁道具まで揃えた本格的な専門店もあります。

ロンドンっ子は haberdashery (イギリス英語では雑貨小物屋さん) という言葉が大好き。北米ではしばしば、帽子やネクタイなどを扱う紳士洋品店を意味する言葉として使われますが、イギリスでは洋裁の材料、特にボタンや糸などを扱う、宝箱のようなお店を意味します。シティ・オブ・ロンドンの 12 の同業者組合団体のひとつ、The Haberdashers' Livery Company は新旧の組合やギルドの集まりで、なかには 14 世紀にまで遡る組合もあります。その会員たちは歴史的に、ボタンやリボン、ピン、ビーズ、そしてその他の雑貨などを売って生計を立ててきました。16 世紀に帽子屋の組合によって組織化され、そのあとで帽子屋の組織と、雑貨小物屋の組織へと別れていきました。

こういった豊かな歴史に溢れているところが、私たちがロンドン、そしてイギリスに惹かれてやまない大きな理由となっています。建築からアートまで、踏みしめる石畳にも、昔話や想像力を掻き立てる歴史に溢れています。ロンドンはイギリスの玄関口として、そしてイギリスのテキスタイルアートの入り口として最適な場所でもあります。シェットランド、フェアアイル、アラン、その他多くのゆかりの場所があります。そしてもちろん、羊！イギリスで飼われている羊の種類は 60 以上にのぼり、これは他のどの国よりも多くなっています。ウール愛好家として、これ以上の場所はあるでしょうか。

他の繊維が素晴らしくないわけではないのですが、イギリスではとにかくウールが王様です。ウールの長い歴史と伝統がイギリス文化の DNA に組み込まれており、いまだに毛糸屋さんも「ウールショップ」と呼ばれているほど。国産のウールを使った英国製の商品、特にウール製品にたいするプライドにはすごいものがあります。Knit British (イギリス的に編もう) という名前のポッドキャストあり、Wovember (11 月の November と Wool をかけた言葉) という社会活動、ウールやその伝統を盛り立てる Shetland Wool Week など、国を挙げてテキスタイルアートを振興しているのです。

Fringe - see page 22 for details.

celebration of the fibre arts.

If you don't have a chance to get round the whole country, London is a great place to start. Our top tip: use public transport to navigate the city. You can cover a lot of ground in a surprisingly short amount of time, as our participants on the Great London Yarn Crawl do. We use the Citymapper app to plan the timings for the routes and it works a treat.

If time constraints are an issue, then pick one or two areas to concentrate on and make plans to come back to what you've missed on your next trip!

イギリス全土を回るチャンスがない場合は、なんでも揃っているロンドンからまず始めるのがいいでしょう。私たちのアドバイスは、とにかく公共交通機関を使うこと。ヤーンクロールの参加者たちが実践している通り、短い時間で驚くほどあちこちを回ることができますよ。Citymapper というアプリを使ってルートを計画しているのですが、電車の時間などもわかって本当に便利です。

時間があまりない場合は、1 つか 2 つのエリアに絞って重点的に回り、また次回ぜひロンドンを訪れる計画を立ててくださいね！

Yarn Shops

毛糸ショップ巡り

LOOP

Loop is probably the most well-known of London's yarn shops. Tucked away on the cobbled street of Camden Passage in North London's Islington and a short walk from Angel tube station, Loop is a calm oasis filled with charming notions, luxury yarns and rare, hard-to-find imports such as Quince & Co., Brooklyn Tweed, and Woolfolk. Owner Susan has built a beautiful shop that overflows with inspiration. In addition to the luxury imports, there is a wide selection of magazines, patterns and books (be sure to check out Loop's 10, in celebration of the shop's 10th anniversary), and local British yarns include Jamieson's, Old Maiden Aunt, Eden Cottage Yarns and The Border Mill, among others.

Loop はおそらくロンドンの毛糸屋さんで一番有名な場所でしょう。北ロンドンのイスリントンに位置する石畳のカムデン通りの一角、Angel という地下鉄の駅から徒歩ですぐのところにあります。可愛い道具、ラグジュアリーな毛糸、珍しく中々手に入らない輸入糸などで溢れる、静かなオアシスのような場所。Quince & Co.、Brooklyn Tweed、Woolfolk などを扱っています。このインスピレーション溢れる美しいお店を作ったのは、オーナーのスーザン。高級な輸入糸に加え、たくさんの雑誌やパターン、書籍などが並んでいます。（Loop's 10 という 10 周年記念のオリジナル本は必見ですよ。）Jamieson's や Old Maiden Aunt、Eden Cottage Yarns、The Border Mill といったイギリスの毛糸も手に入ります。

WILD & WOOLLY

Head east into Hackney and you'll find Wild & Woolly, where owner Anna can be found putting the kettle on. This tiny shop makes incredible use of space and is filled to the rafters with strong, workhorse yarn with a mostly local and British bent. Yarns include Kalinka linen by Karin Oberg, hand-dyed treats from London dyers Travelknitter, The Wool Kitchen and EasyKnits, and British gems such as Townhouse Alpacas and Baa Ram Ewe. Check their schedule for their monthly knit night lock-ins where you'll meet some of the friendliest knitters ever!

ハックニー通りを東に向かうと、Wild & Woolly でやかんを火にかけるオーナーのアナと出会えます。この小さなショップは空間を驚くほど有効に使い、その多くが英国産の、日常使いに手頃な毛糸が天井までぎっしりと詰まっています。Karin Oberg の Kalinka リネンや、Travelknitter、The Wool Kitchen、EasyKnits などロンドンの手染め糸、そして Townhouse Alpacas や Baa Ram Ewe といった素敵なイギリスの毛糸などにお目にかかれます。毎月行われているニットナイトでは、とってもフレンドリーな編みもの仲間たちと出会えるので、ぜひスケジュールをチェックして参加してみてくださいね。

KNIT WITH ATTITUDE

Also in Hackney and part of the East London Triangle (W&W is a member too), Knit With Attitude showcases owner Maya's passion for eco-friendly and ethically sourced yarns. Yarns are primarily from small British and European companies and extend to brands from further afield that can be traced back to independent and family-run businesses. Knit With Attitude also shares their shop with Of Cabbages and Kings, a gallery with gifts and wares from local Hackney makers and artists.

東ロンドン・トライアングル（3 店舗）の 1 つ、これもハックニー通りにあるお店です（W&W もその 1 つ）。Knit With Attitude はオーナーであるマヤの情熱あふれるセレクションが特徴。環境に優しく、エシカルに作られた毛糸が集まっています。ほとんどの毛糸がイギリスやヨーロッパの小さいメーカーのもので、その他、家族経営で作られているような海外のブランドもあります。Of Cabbages and Kings という、ハックニー界隈のアーティスト作品を集めたギャラリー兼ギフトショップと店舗を共有しています。

Loop - see page 16 & 22 for details.

THE VILLAGE HABERDASHERY

If you love fabric as much as you love yarn you'll want to check out The Village Haberdashery in West Hampstead. The shop recently relocated to a larger space and has expanded to fill it with more yarns, fabrics, patterns and more. They also have a fantastic selection of stationery, ribbons, trims, zippers and buttons. Be sure to look up their class schedule as they often have special guest tutors such as Great British Sewing Bee 2016 winner Charlotte Newland, and quilting experts Anna Maria Horner and Lizzy House.

STAG & BOW

Head south and east across the city to Forest Hill and you'll find Stag & Bow. This friendly shop is all about making and carries the materials to do so, as well as handmade items by local artisans. You can find yarns, fabric and haberdashery at Stag & Bow, as well as classes ranging from indigo dyeing to weaving and more.

もし毛糸だけでなくファブリックも好きだったら、ウエスト・ハムステッドにある The Village Haberdashery をお勧めします。最近大きな場所へ移転したこのお店、毛糸や生地、パターンの取り扱い点数がさらに増えました。また、文具やリボン、縁飾り、ファスナー、ボタンなども多数扱っています。Great British Sewing Bee 2016 というソーイングコンテストの優勝者、シャーロット・ニューランド、アメリカンキルトの第一人者アナ・マリア・ホーマー (ナッシュヴィルの特集で紹介した Craft South のオーナー)、リジー・ハウスなど、有名なゲストを招待してのワークショップが頻繁に行われているので、お店のカレンダーをチェックしてから行くと良いでしょう。

ロンドンの街を南東に横切ると、フォレスト・ヒルというエリアに Stag & Bow があります。この親しみやすいお店はとにかく手作りに関するものが揃う場所。それに加え、地元の作家が作ったアイテムなども扱っています。毛糸、ファブリック、ボタンやリボンなどが買え、藍染から手織りまで、様々なワークショップに参加することができます。

DAY TRIP DESTINATION FOR CRAFTERS - BATH, UK

バースへ日帰りクラフトの旅

London is a fantastic gateway to the rest of the country and you can see a surprising amount in daytrips from the city. One of our favourites is to Bath, an short 90-minute train ride from London's famous Paddington Station. If you love history, architecture and Jane Austen then Bath has you covered in more ways than one! All of Bath has been designated a UNESCO World Heritage City. It's also a compact place and most sights are easily walkable from the train station. Here's some of our favourites:

ロンドンはイギリス各地への玄関口として、本当に様々な１日ツアーが企画されています。その中でも私たちのお気に入りの目的地はバース、ロンドンの有名なパディントン駅からたった１時間半の距離にあります。歴史や建築、ジェーン・オースティンが好きだったら、バースに行けばそのすべてが揃っています！バース全域が UNESCO の世界遺産に登録されています。また、とてもコンパクトな街で、ほとんどの観光地が駅からの徒歩圏にあります。私たちのオススメの場所を紹介しますよ。

WOOL, COUNTRY THREADS

A short, 10-minute walk from the train station are Wool and Country Threads. Both shops are tucked away on the same cobblestone laneway, just opposite each other, and each are filled with yarns and fabrics galore. Country Threads is full of ribbons and buttons too. Be sure to visit their back room which has even more fabrics! Wool boasts British stalwart brands such as Debbie Bliss and Rowan with other treats hidden on their shelves as well.

Wool, Country Threads

駅から徒歩 10 分で行けるのは、Wool と Country Threads という２店。どちらも同じ石畳の路地に、ほぼ向かい合わせにあり、いずれも毛糸やファブリックが所狭しと並んでいます。Country Threads にはリボンやボタンもあります。お店の奥の部屋に入るのを忘れずに！もっとファブリックが詰まっていますよ。Wool には Debbie Bliss や Rowan といったイギリスの定番毛糸から、棚の隙間に詰まった珍しい毛糸まで色々あります。

ONE TWO FIVE GALLERY

Fabric artist and designer Carole Waller and her ceramicist husband Gary Wood have their gallery on Abbey Green, located in the shadow of Bath Abbey. If you're looking for a special gift you'll find it here; with Carole's hand painted silk scarves and clothes, and Gary's pottery.

One Two Five Gallery

手芸作家でテキスタイルデザイナーのカロル・ワラーと、陶芸家のご主人ゲーリー・ウッドが運営するギャラリーで、バース寺院の傍のアビー・グリーン通りにあります。珍しいギフトを探しているなら、カロルの手染めのシルクスカーフや洋服、ゲーリーの器はいかがでしょうか。

BATH ABBEY, THE ROMAN BATHS

Located in the same square are Bath's most famous attractions, the towering Abbey and the Roman Baths. Both are must-sees for the architecture alone, and the Roman Baths feature an excellent self-guided tour. For those wanting to partake of Bath's natural thermal waters, bookings can be made at the nearby Thermae Bath Spa.

バース寺院とローマ・バス

街の同じ区画にある、バースで最も有名な観光地の２つ、巨大な寺院とローマ時代の遺跡です。どちらも、その建築的価値だけでもみどころがあり、ローマ・バスではセルフガイドツアーが秀逸です。バースで温泉に入ってみたい場合は、近くに Thermae Bath Spa があり、予約できますよ。

A YARN STORY, ARTISAN QUARTER

Wander beyond the Abbey and you'll find yourself in Bath's Artisan Quarter. Walcot

A Yarn Story と Artisan Quarter

寺院を越えると、バースの Artisan Quarter（アーティスト地区）が見えてきます。ウォルコット通りにはギャ

A Yarn Story

Wool

Street stretches with an eclectic mix of galleries, cafes, studios and shops of local makers and artists. Also on Walcot Street is A Yarn Story, purveyors of fine yarns from around the world such as Shibui, SweetGeorgia, Julie Asselin, The Fibre Co. and their own line, Walcot Yarns.

FASHION MUSEUM BATH, THE ASSEMBLY ROOMS

Created with the single donation of one woman's collection of fashion costume pieces, the Fashion Museum Bath is an amazing collection of historic and contemporary clothing. It also boasts an incredible archive of knitting and crochet patterns which can often be visited privately in small groups. Check with the museum for more details. Admission also includes access to the Assembly Rooms, a stunning example of Georgian architecture.

JANE AUSTEN CENTRE

The Jane Austen Centre celebrates Bath's most famous resident and provides an insight into what it was like to live in Regency times. The Centre features an exhibition as well as opportunities to try on Regency dresses and bonnets. There's also a tea room with a rooftop view of Bath.

NO. 1 ROYAL CRESCENT

One of Bath's original Georgian town houses, No. 1 Royal Crescent offers a snapshot of what life would have been like in Georgian Bath. The rooms have been restored to show how they would have looked to wealthy visitors coming to take the waters. Every detail has been seen to, including below stairs in the kitchen, scullery and servants' quarters.

ラリーやカフェ、アーティストのスタジオや、地元の作家の作品を扱うお店などが集まっています。ウォルコット通りにはまた、Shibui や Sweet Georgia、Julie Asselin、The Fibre Co. など、世界中から集められた良質な毛糸と、オリジナルの毛糸 Walcot Yarns を扱う A Yarn Story があります。

バースファッション博物館とアセンブリー・ルーム

ある 1 人の女性のコレクション寄贈だけで設立された、バースのファッション博物館。歴史的な衣装から現代のファッションまで、素晴らしい作品の数々をみることができます。ここにはまた膨大な数の棒針やかぎ針のパターンが所蔵されており、少人数のグループでプライベートツアーを予約することが可能です。詳細は博物館に問い合わせをお願いします。チケットにはアセンブリー・ルームという、ジョージ王朝時代の傑作建築の拝観料も含まれます。

ジェーン・オースティン・センター

ジェーン・オースティン・センターはバースの最も有名な住人と、摂政時代の暮らしぶりを紹介する場所です。本センターでは企画展や常設展を行なっており、そしてその時代のドレスや帽子などを試着することもできます。バースを上から眺められるティールームもオススメです。

ロイヤル・クレセント 1 番地

バースに最初に作られたジョージ王朝時代のタウンハウスの 1 つ、ロイヤル・クレセント 1 番地は、その当時の生活を垣間見させてくれる場所です。バースに湯治に訪れる裕福な人々が当時使っていた部屋の様子が、建物の中には復元されています。細部までこだわられていて、キッチンの階下、食器洗い場や使用人の部屋まで当時の通りとなっています。

London with Susan Cropper

Essey by Susan Cropper

人気毛糸店 Loop London のオーナー、スーザン・クロッパーのお気に入り

London, my home for the past 31 years after leaving NYC, is a gorgeous multi-cultural city steeped in history. At the same time, London continues to inspire with the very best of new theatre, arts, music and craft alongside loads of great parks. It's an amazing place for anyone interested in knitting, textiles and fibre-arts! From museums like the Victoria and Albert and the wonderful small independent shops to the very fabric you sit on getting to these places - it is chock-full of inspiration.

I opened Loop 12 years ago and have aimed to make it resemble the best yarn fair in the world. We have loads of gorgeous yarns in natural fibres and hand-dyes from small artisanal UK-based yarn dyers, and from around the world. Alongside incredible vintage and handmade haberdashery, we also stock the work of textile artists such as Sophie Digard, Nathalie Lete and Julie Arkell.

I so hope you enjoy your London trip and find lots of inspiration! Here are a few of my favourite places and things to do in this big, wonderful city.

THE ROYAL ACADEMY

This is a favourite art museum of mine. I love looking at the beautifully curated contemporary exhibitions in their ornate old rooms.

FORTNUM & MASONS

A food mecca for over 300 years and home of the most beautiful packaging you can find.

Just nearby is Chinatown, the place to go for Dim Sum as well as my favourite cinema in London, **The Picturehouse Central**, which also has a terrific cafe and shows great independent films. The perfect combination for a rainy Sunday afternoon!

The ribbon empire of London, **VV Rouleaux**, is tucked away on a side street on Marylebone Lane, and has the most incredible selection of ribbons and small textile treasures.

ニューヨークを後にし 31 年前に移り住んだロンドンは、歴史が染み付いた美しい国際都市です。と同時に、ロンドンは新しい演劇、芸術、音楽や工芸の粋を集めて人々を魅了し続け、また素晴らしい公園もたくさんあります。編みものやテキスタイル、ファイバーアートに興味がある人にとっては、本当に絶好の場所です。ヴィクトリア・アルバート博物館のような美術館・博物館、個人経営の美しいショップ、そしてそこに向かう地下鉄のシートに使われている生地まで、刺激に満ち溢れています。

Loop を開店したのは 12 年前、それ以来というもの、世界で一番の毛糸ショップを目指して努力を重ねてきました。天然繊維の美しい毛糸から、イギリスや世界中の染色家たちが染めた毛糸まで、沢山揃えています。ビンテージ物や手作りの素材に加え、ソフィー・ディガードやナタリー・レテ、ジュリー・アーケルといったアーティストの作品も扱っています。

そんな Loop があるロンドン。皆さんもこの街での滞在を楽しみ、沢山刺激をもらえますように。この巨大で素晴らしい街の、私なりの楽しみかたやお気に入りの場所を紹介します。

ロイヤル・アカデミー

私のお気に入りの美術館です。美しくキュレーションされた現代アートの展覧会を、装飾に富んだ古い部屋で見るのが大好きです。

フォートナム＆メイソン

300 年続く食材のメッカであり、この世の美しい包装・パッケージングが結集した場所です。

飲茶をよく食べにいく**チャイナタウン**のほど近くに、好きな映画館、**The Picturehouse Central** があります。ここは素敵なカフェも併設していて、いつもいいインディペンデント映画を上映しています。雨の日曜の午後にはぴったりの組み合わせ！

ロンドンのリボンの王国、**VV Rouleaux** はメアリルボーン・レーンの脇道にひっそりとあります。リボンやテキスタイルの宝物の見事なコレクションがありますよ。

Photos courtesy of Loop London.

The whole area of **Marylebone High Street** is a favourite haunt of mine as it's an incredibly lovely shopping (and eating!) street, home to **Designer's Guild** (home textiles), **Skandium** (Scandinavian home decor), **Aesop, Daunt Books** and a special little ceramic shop called **Eclectic66**, where I treat myself once in a while to their amazing Japanese ceramics.

CLOTH HOUSE

They source beautiful, mostly natural fabrics and haberdashery from all over the world, sometimes working closely with local textile traders and artisans and using traditional skills.

Spitalfields Market and Shoreditch are both great places to wander.

LOOP AND CAMDEN PASSAGE, ISLINGTON

My favourite place to be is Loop, located in the great neighbourhood of Islington. Loop is on wonderful Camden Passage, a pedestrian way filled with vintage and antique shops, more cafes - including my favourite **The Elk in the Woods** - and lots of other independent shops.

For addresses and contact details, please see the list and map on page 22-23.

All information was correct at the time of writing this but it is always best to either call or check websites for up-to-date opening hours and information to avoid any disappointment.

このメアリルボーン・ハイストリート地区全体は、ショッピングに、そして食事に最高のお店ばかりで、お気に入りの散策場所です。**デザイナーズギルド**（ホームテキスタイル）、**スカンディウム**（北欧のインテリア）、**Aesop**、**Daunt Books**（世界で最も美しい書店に選ばれたお店）、そして、時々自分へのご褒美にと日本の器を買ってしまう、**Eclectic66** という小さくて素敵な陶器屋さんもあります。

Cloth House

世界中からとても美しい、天然素材の生地や雑貨を集めたお店で、時にはその地域の伝統的な技法を用いたアーティストやメーカーの商材も扱っています。

Old Spitalfields Market やショーディッチ地区も歩き回るのに最高のエリアです。

イスリングトンの Loop とカムデン通り

イスリングトンの素敵な界隈にある Loop はもちろん、私の特にお気に入りの場所です。カムデン通りはビンテージ物やアンティークを扱うお店が集まる歩行者天国の通りで、カフェもたくさんあります。私が好きなのは The Elk in the Woods というお店。他にも個人経営の素敵なお店が立ち並びます。

住所と詳細は 22-23 ページの地図とリストを参照してください。

すべての情報は本記事執筆時点のものであり、訪問前にはウェブサイトをチェックしたり電話したりして、最新の営業時間や住所を確認することをオススメします。

London Craft Map

1. Drink, Shop & Do
This café near to Kings Cross features and ever-changing line up of creative workshops and special events.
常に色々な手作り WS やイベントを行なっているカフェ。
9 Caledonian Road, Kings Cross London N1 9DX
(closest tube: King's Cross)
www.drinkshopdo.co.uk

2. Fabrications
The third point in the East London Triangle, Fabrications is an independent shop, gallery and studio dedicated to upcycling and eco design.
東ロンドン・トライアングルの3つめ、アップサイクルに焦点を当てたギャラリーショップ。
7 Broadway Market, Hackney London E8 4PH
(closest tube: Cambridge Heath)
www.fabrications1.co.uk

3. Fringe
Yarn, fabric and haberdashery shop in North London that also doubles as a gallery space with regular exhibitions, pop-ups and workshops.
北ロンドンの手芸ショップ、貸しスペースとして展示会なども行う。
108 Alexandra Park Road, Muswell Hill, London N10 2AE
(closest tube: Bounds Green)
www.fringe108.london

4. Goldhawk Road (for fabrics)
More of a general destination than a single shop, Goldhawk Road is lined with fabric shops. Great bargains to be found here if you're good with taking your time exploring.
日本の日暮里のような生地街。探索すると掘り出し物も。
(closest tube: Goldhawk Road or Shepherd's Bush)

5. The Good Yarn Stall
Only found on Sundays in Spitalfields Market near Leon between 10am and 5pm.
Spitalfields Market に日曜日の10時~5時だけ出店する毛糸店。
(closest tube: Shoreditch High St)
www.thegoodyarnstall.co.uk

6. The Handweavers Studio & Gallery
Weavers and spinners will be delighted to explore the treasure trove found here! Yarns include wool and natural fibres as well as specialty yarns such as raffia, metal blends, iridescent and reflective yarns and more.
織りや紡ぎの材料が豊富に揃う。
140 Seven Sisters Road, London N7 7NS
(closest tube: Finsbury Park)
www.handweavers.co.uk

7. I Knit London
The shop carries a varied selection of yarns including in-house I Knit or Dye, dyed by owner Gerard.
オーナーのジェラルドが手染めした毛糸を始め、様々な毛糸を扱う。
106 Lower Marsh, London SE1 7AB
(closest: Waterloo Station)
iknit.org.uk

8. Knit With Attitude
Details on page 16. 16 ページ参照
127 Stoke Newington High Street London N16 0PH
(closest tube: Stoke Newington)
www.knitwithattitude.com

9. Knit Works London
Specialty shop focused on workshops and machine-knitting with yarns. Owner Tim is extremely knowledgeable and machines can also be booked by the hour.
機械編みに特化したお店で、機械をお店で使うことも可能。
Unit 12, Palmers Road, Bethnal Green, London E2 0SY
(closest tube: Mile End)
www.knitworkslondon.com

London Craft Club (10)
Creators of mini workshops and corporate events, class offerings run from decoupage to jewellery-making or even making your own espadrilles! A great way to try something new. Check their calendar for the latest listings.
色々なクラフトの WS をロンドンの複数の場所で展開。Web のカレンダーをチェックして。
www.londoncraftclub.co.uk

11. The London Loom
A new weaving space in Hackney, east London with a focus on freestyle weaving and exploring with texture. Workshops use either a tapestry or simple two pedal floor loom.
ハックニーエリアの新しい手織りスタジオ。WS が受けられる。
Studio 8, Hackney Downs Studios 17 Amhurst Terrace, London E8 2BT
(closest tube: Rectory Road)
www.thelondonloom.com

12. Loop
Details on page 16. 16 ページ参照 .
15 Camden Passage Islington, London N1 8EA
(closest tube: Angel)
www.loopknittingshop.com

The Make Escape (13)
Host of monthly maker evenings in Hackney with special guests, free entry, DJ and bar. Check their blog for more details.
フリーのクラフトイベントを月1会開催。詳細はブログを確認。
themakeescape.blogspot.co.uk

14. Nest
A sweet yarn and fabric shop located in London's Crouch End. Yarns include Erika Knight, Bergere de France and Blue Sky Fibers.
毛糸と生地を扱う可愛らしいお店。Erika Knight や Bergere de France など。
102 Weston Park, London N8 9PP
(closest tube: Hornsey)
www.nestknitting.com

15. Ray Stitch
Incredibly stylish sewing and fabric shop in Islington. In addition to beautiful fabrics, buttons and haberdashery, Ray Stitch offers an excellent selection of patterns and staff are friendly and knowledgeable. They also have excellent workshops.
スタイリッシュな生地屋。スタッフも知識豊富で、良い WS が受けられる。
66-68 Essex Road, London N1 8LR
(closest tube: Essex Road)
www.raystitch.co.uk

16. Sharp Works
The Herne Hill's LYS offers a wide range of yarns from Debbie Bliss and Rowan to Manos and Mirasol and more. This crochet-friendly shop also has a good selection of notions and haberdashery. Only open Wednesday through Saturday.
Rowan やその他輸入糸、道具など扱う毛糸ショップ。水曜~土曜開店。
220 Railton Road, Herne Hill London SE24 0JT
(closest station: Herne Hill)
www.sharpworks.co.uk

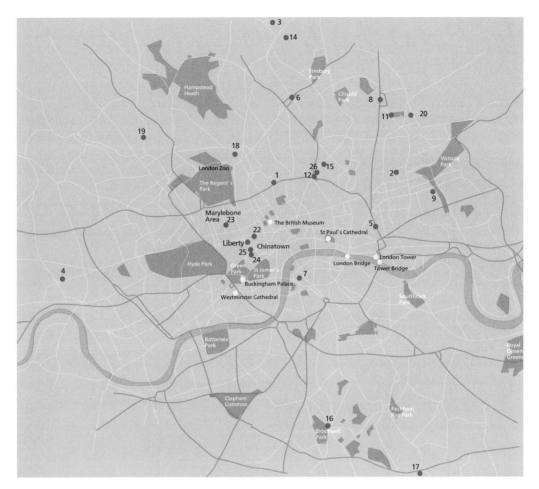

17. Stag & Bow
Details on page 17. 17 ページ参照 .
8 Dartmouth Road
Forest Hill, London SE23 3XU
(closest station: Forest Hill)
stagandbow.com

18. Tea and Crafting
Organisers of workshops and
hen parties in a range of crafts
from embroidery to 3D-printed
jewellery. Classes are limited
to 6-8 people for an intimate
experience and take place in
either Camden Town or Covent
Garden.
刺繍から 3D プリンターを使ったア
クセサリーまで、様々なクラフトの
WS を主催。場所は 2 箇所なので
Web をチェック。
www.teaandcrafting.co.uk

19. The Village Haberdashery
Details on page 17. 17 ページ参照 .
West Hampstead Square, London
NW6 2BR
(closest tube: West Hampstead)
www.thevillagehaberdashery.
co.uk

20. Wild & Woolly
Details on page 16. 16 ページ参照 .
116 Lower Clapton Road, London
E5 0QR
(closest station: Hackney Central)
www.wildandwoollyshop.co.uk

The Workbench (21)
A combination of cocktails and
custom, handcrafted jewellery
are the attraction with these
pop-up workshops held monthly
across London. Projects are
carved from jewellers' wax
before being transformed into
solid silver and delivered a few
weeks later.
ロンドン各地で行われるジュエリー
制作の WS。制作後、数週間で完成
品を受け取れる。Web から予約を。
www.theworkbenchlondon.com

22. Cloth House
Details on page 21. 21 ページ参照 .
47 Berwick Street, W1
(closest tube: Oxford Circus)
www.clothhouse.com

23. VV Rouleaux
Details on page 20. 20 ページ参照 .
102 Marylebone Lane, W1
(closest tube: Oxford Circus or
Bond St)
www.vvrouleaux.com

24. Fortnum & Masons
Details on page 20. 20 ページ参照 .
181 Piccadilly, W1
(closest tube either Piccadilly
Circus or Green Park)
www.fortnumandmason.com/
restaurants/diamond-jubilee-
tea-salon

25. The Royal Academy
Details on page 20. 20 ページ参照 .
Burlington House, Piccadilly, W1
(closest tube either Piccadilly
Circus or Green Park)
www.royalacademy.org.uk

26. Elk in the Woods
Details on page 21. 21 ページ参照 .
37 Camden Passage, N1
(closest tube: Angel)
www.the-elk-in-the-woods.co.uk

The Great London Yarn Crawl

グレート・ロンドン・ヤーンクロールと Yarn In The City

The Great London Yarn Crawl is Yarn in the City's annual charity event benefitting Refuge. Held annually at the beginning of September, the event kicks off the autumn knitting season with 150 yarn enthusiasts exploring yarn, fabric and haberdashery shops around London on a pre-determined route. Following a day of yarn-y sights, participants come together for an after-party for door prizes and a chance to show off their wares and drop off hand knits for Knit for Peace.

November 2018 will see the return of Yarn in the City's biennial yarn show, Yarnporium. The Yarnporium is a two-day event celebrating sweater weather, yarn, fibre, friends and the making community. Yarnporium also includes the Indie Maker Spotlight with new and emerging indie-dyers and makers as well as workshops from well-known knitting and crochet designers from across the UK. Save the date now for November 2-3, 2018!

The Great London Yarn Crawl はロンドンで毎年行われるチャリティーイベントで、収益は難民支援に当てられます。9月の最初にあり、秋の編みものシーズンの開始を告げるイベントとして、150人ほどの編みもの愛好家がロンドンの毛糸屋、生地屋さんや手芸雑貨店を決められたルートにしたがって回ります。1日毛糸屋を回った後はパーティに集まり、賞品をゲットしたり、着ているものを自慢しあったり、Knit for Peace に編んだものを寄付したりします。

2018年11月には2年に1度のイベント、Yarnporium が開催されます。これはセーターを着るシーズンの到来や、毛糸、そして編みもののコミュニティを祝う2日間のイベントです。Yarnporium ではまた、新しい毛糸の染色家や個人の作家さんをフィーチャーしたり、イギリス全土の有名なニットやかぎ針作品のデザイナーを紹介したりします。2018年11月2～3日は要チェックです！

YARN IN THE CITY

Rachel and Allison have also written the London Craft Guide, a guidebook with over 30 profiles of yarn, fabric and haberdashery shops from around the city. Suggestions are included for day trips and the book also includes patterns for knitting, crochet and sewing projects that can be started right away while on holiday.

ロンドンの30以上のお店を網羅した London Craft Guide を出版したレイチェルとアリソンの2人組。ガイドには日帰りで行けるオススメの場所や、お休みの日に簡単にできる棒針、かぎ針、ソーイングのプロジェクトなども載っています。

LON-DON CRAFT GUIDE

YARN IN THE CITY

London, Pink

This collection of warm garments and accessories, all in pink's many hues, keep you cozy while exploring London.
ロンドンを旅する気分で着る、温かなピンク系のウェアと小物8点。

Gneiss

Fiona Alice

A top-down pullover knit in two colors of hand-dyed yarn, using the Intarsia technique. The combination of speckled and dark grey semi-solid yarns from La Bien Aimée makes it look like a beautiful Gneiss. Choosing high-contrasting colors is recommended. It's such a fun garment to make!

二色の手染め糸をインターシアの技法で編むトップダウンセーター。La Bien Amiée のカラフルな speckled(斑点状に染められている糸) とダークな単色糸との組み合わせがまるで美しい岩石のように見えることから Gneiss と名付けられました。コントラストの効いた色選びがポイント。前後の模様、そして編み方の違いなど、楽しい要素たっぷりのセーターです。

Devon

Paula Pereira

A top-down pullover with twisted ribbing. Brooklyn Tweed Shelter helps keep the garment light and fitted, even though it's knit entirely in ribbing. Short rows are added to back yoke and hem for creating extra comfort. Wear it with your favorite pair of denim, and go for a walk without a jacket on deep fall's chilly days..

リブ編みのトップダウンセーター。全体がリブ編み模様である割に、軽く、そして体に程よくフィットするのは Brooklyn Tweed の Shelter のおかげ。後ろヨークと裾に引返しを加え、着やすい 1 枚になっています。寒い日にパッとジーンズの上に着て出掛けられる、頼れる 1 枚になるはずです。

Kew

Nele Redweik

A hat with bold botanical motifs on the sides, inspired by cloche hats from the 1920s. While Brooklyn Tweed Arbor gives the hat a solid structure, a silk mohair yarn adds softness - it would be interesting to play with different color combinations.

ボタニカルモチーフが印象的な帽子。 1920 年代に流行ったクローシェをイメージしたデザインです。 Isager の Silk Mohair と Brooklyn Tweed の Arbor の組み合わせがほどよくマッチ、モヘアとウールの色合いを変えることで、色々遊べそうな 1 枚です。

Bavaria

Isabell Kraemer

Knit in garter stitch and bobbles, this asymmetrical triangular wrap is made with sensuous Quince and Co. Owl.

It can be your go-to snuggle wrap for drafty old houses and chilly winter car rides.

Quince & Co. の Owl のやわらかい質感を思う存分楽しめる大判ショール。ガーターと二つのボッブル模様を繰り返しながらアシンメトリーな三角形を作っていきます。寒い季節、車や家の中での必需品アイテムになることでしょう。

Pink Pine Pair

Nataliya Sinelshchikova

A pair of mittens with symmetrically laid-out triangles. The many techniques used in this petite project will keep you engaged. Choosing a bright color for this accessory adds a vibrant pop to an otherwise gloomy winter wardrobe. It would also make a great holiday gift.

左右対称にデザインされた三角形模様のミトン。小さなアイテムですが、インターシア、ねじり模様と技法が満載な1枚です。コントラストの効いた2色を選ぶのがおすすめ。ダークな色合いの多い、冬の装いのアクセントにぜひ。プレゼントにも最適ですよ。

Ostinato

Camille Rosselle

Knit in GENMOU from DARUMA, this basic pullover has all-over texture and I-Cord details. The combination of GENMOU with the stitch pattern creates an interesting effect. You will finish this pullover in no time while enjoying its texture. A great piece for fall layering.

DARUMA の GENMOU で編む、シンプルな形の プルオーバー。全面を地模様で編み、襟ぐり以外 を I-Cord で仕上げます。ボコボコしたステッチを GENMOU のふんわりとした糸で編むことで面白いテ クスチャが生まれ、編み地を楽しみながらすいすい編 めそう。お好きな色で秋の 1 枚を。

Sunday Market

Ayano Tanaka

A seamless bottom-up pullover full of clever details. Body and sleeves have slipped stitch detail, while the flared shape adds whimsy to the design. It's a quick knit with worsted-weight yarn. Pair it with your favorite skirts or fitted denim pants.

ボトムアップで編むシンプルなセーター。身頃と袖上に入った引上げ模様がポイントで、裾のＡラインで可愛さをプラス。ざっくり編んで、スカートでもパンツでも気楽に着られる１枚です。

Raindrops

Mizuho Komiya

We chose a vivid orange-red in Hedgehog Fibers for this cowl, an eye-catching accent for a dark winter jacket. Choose two contrasting colors for the maximum effect. This pattern is scattered with an array of sweet raindrops and the cowl can be worn single or doubled.

雨粒模様が可愛い、ドーナツ型カウル。コントラストの効いた 2 色を選べば、はっきりとした雨粒が現れます。Hedgehog Fibers の楽しい明るめの色で編めば、冬の装いのアクセントになりますよ。1 重でも 2 重にしても使えるのが嬉しいところ。

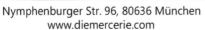

The story of GENMOU

DARUMA's new yarn, GENMOU, debuts this fall

GENMOU が海を渡るまで。

In Japan, everyone knows DARUMA for their hand sewing thread. Most of us grew up seeing our grandmothers and mothers sewing kimonos or kitchen towels with DARUMA thread. It is such a small household item, yet memorable, probably thanks to the unusual trademark and its quality. The trademark, Daruma, is the 6th century priest who started Zen Buddhism in China. He is often portrayed in a round shape, because the legend says he lost his limbs from continuing Zen meditation for 9 years. The red, round shape with an often comical face is regarded as a symbol for achieving your goals after hard work.

Now, DARUMA Yarn. It is a less common knowledge that they also manufacture knitting yarn. Most of their products had been a mass-produced type for craft store chains, until several years ago, when the product development head at that time, and now current President, decided that it was about time to do things differently. While many Japanese

ダルマ糸といえば日本では手縫い糸の印象が強力です。祖母や母の裁縫道具箱に入っている手縫い糸のダルママークや、それで着物や布巾などを縫う姿を見て育ったという方々も多いでしょう。家庭の中ではほんの小さいものですが、なぜか印象深いのは、変わった（ちょっと怖い）ダルママークによるのではないかと思います。ブランドのトレードマークとなっている達磨、6世紀に中国で禅宗を広めたという僧侶が起源です。丸い姿で表現されるのは、9年間座禅を続けているうちに手足が腐ってなくなってしまったという話が伝わっているからなのだとか。その赤く丸いかたち、そしてコミカルな顔は、今では努力の末に目標を叶えることのシンボルとなっています。

さて、DARUMA の毛糸。この会社がウールの毛糸を作り出したのはここ数年の話です。かつてはほとんどの商品が量販店向けのアクリル 100% の毛糸でしたが、数年前から様子が変わってきました。当時企画室長だった現在の社長さんが、このままではいけないと思い切って舵を切ったところから始まりました。毎年、日本の毛糸メーカーの多くが新商品として新しい糸を発表している中で、質の良い、他社メーカーにはない商品を作ろうという挑戦が始まりました。原毛に近い

yarn makers release new yarns every year, they decided to pursue quality and to create unique products. GENMOU is one of these new products, created in an effort to design a yarn that is as light and soft as it could be. "It's easy to make a light yarn if you mix acrylics, but we didn't want to do that. The idea we came up with was to use carded wool." Nylon threads are often used for holding a string of roving together, but for GENMOU yarn DARUMA created a thread from the same wool. When they searched for the source material, the wool had to be soft, high micron and even enough to use as it was, as well as for spinning an extra-thin thread. "GENMOU" means raw wool in Japanese, and was named because touching the yarn reminded the team of touching the soft body of merino sheep.

It was in fall 2014 when DARUMA and amirisu started a discussion on potential collaboration. While amirisu imports many yarns from overseas, bringing high-quality Japanese products to the international fiber market has been one of our goals since setting up the company. The reason why amirisu considered DARUMA special was their impressive vast knowledge in yarn manufacturing - from sourcing to spinning and dyeing. They knew how to make the yarn they want. On the other hand, DARUMA wanted a new and exciting challenge for the next generation of their employees.

DARUMA and amirisu agreed that a yarn like GENMOU is fairly uncommon in both Japanese and international markets, and it is a yarn that DARUMA is planning on expanding in years to come. The yarn is made in Bishu in Aichi Prefecture, the area historically known

メリノウールはそんな時に作られた商品です。できるだけ軽くて柔らかい毛糸を作りたい、というチームの想いから生まれました。「糸を軽くするためにはアクリルなどの合繊を混紡することがいちばん簡単なのですが、手触りを考えると天然繊維100％で作りたいと思いました。そこで思いついたのが、ほとんど撚りをかけずに糸にすることでした。」粗糸（ウールを撚りをかけずに糸状にしたもの）を繋ぎ止めるにはナイロンの糸を巻きつけるのが一般的ですが、原毛に近いメリノウールではそれも同じメリノウールで作りました。その細い糸を作るには、原料のウールも質の良い、とても均質で細いものでないと難しく、現在のものに行き着いたのだとか。原毛という名前をつけたのは、メリノ種の羊を触った時のふっくらとした手触りを思い描いたから。

DARUMAとamirisuが何か一緒にできないか、と話し合いを始めたのは2014年の秋になります。amirisuではたくさんの毛糸を海外から輸入していますが、日本に質の高い商品があればぜひ海外に紹介したいというのが、会社設立当初からの目標のひとつでした。DARUMAの方々と一緒に仕事をするきっかけのひとつは、その商品開発に関する知識の深さ。原料、紡績、染めのあらゆる工程について、本当にたくさんのことを教えていただきました。こんな糸が作りたい、と思ったら、それをどうやって作るかはちゃんと知っている。真剣にものづくりに取り組んでいるメーカーです。一方で、DARUMAは次の世代に向けて、DARUMAにしかできない、ワクワクすることにみんなで取り組みたい、と考えていました。

当時の商品をつぶさに検討した結果、原毛に近いメリノウールのような糸は日本にも海外にもあまりないし、今後力を入れていきたい商品であるということになりました。歴史的に羊毛製品の生産で知られる愛知県の尾州で作られているこの糸。地域には紡績工場や染め工場が集積していて、それらを行き来しながら作られています。日本では30g玉で販売していますが、海外向けに50gにパッケージし直し、GENMOUと

for wool products. Many small mills and dye houses are concentrated in close proximity, and GENMOU is manufactured back and forth between two places. The yarn is sold in a smaller ball in Japan, but has been repackaged as a 50g ball with a brand-new label.

The collection, GENMOU 2017, was put together based on a mood board the team created. "We did not try to make a collection with a Japanese aesthetic, but the designers we invited were inspired by the geometric images and Japanese scenery on the mood board." One of DARUMA's factories was used as a location for the photo shoot, so we could show people how and where they make their products.

GENMOU is the first DARUMA yarn to travel overseas, but definitely not the last. The team wants to continue creating exciting and fun products nobody else makes, and it may not be limited to yarn and thread.

GENMOU yarn and 2017 Collection patterns are available through global stockists and on DARUMA Ravelry store.

新しいロゴの入ったラベルをつけました。

1 年以上かけて準備した GENMOU 2017 コレクション。DARUMA チームのイメージを伝えるために様々な画像を集め、デザイナーさんに伝えるところから始まりました。「特に日本的なコレクションを作りたいとは思っていなかったのですが、参加してくれたデザイナーさんたちは幾何学的な模様や日本の景色に触発された様子でした」と DARUMA。お客様や海外の皆さんに、背景にあるものづくりの現場を感じてもらえればうれしいと、撮影は滋賀の自社工場で行いました。

GENMOU は海外へ紹介する最初の糸となりましたが、今後も挑戦は続きます。これからも他にはない、ワクワクすることをしていきたい、とチームは意気込みます。そして、それは毛糸や糸だけではないかもしれない、と。

原毛に近いウールの海外版、GENMOU は amirisu を通じて海外の毛糸ショップへ、そしてお客様へ届けられています。2017 年コレクションは Ravelry で、そして日本語版は amirisu で翻訳し販売します。

Photo on page 53 by Kotori Kawashima; photos on page 54-55 courtesy of DARUMA.

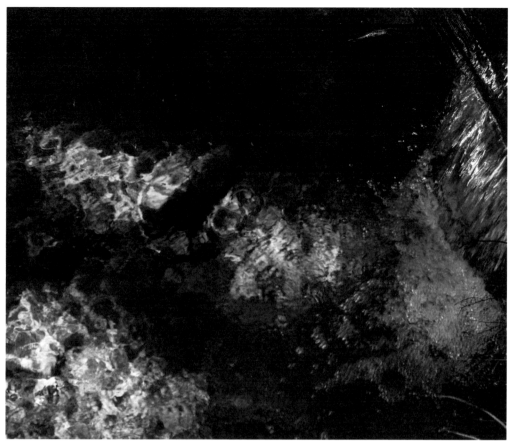

In the fall, I often take to the woods again. The colors and shadows intensify. The leaves drop from the trees and the forest opens up. I took this photograph on a walk at a nearby national park on a little side trail that isn't visited very often by tourists. The air was noticeably cooler than the day before, as I stood by the creek and watched the light play on the surface of the water. It was a quiet moment, just me and my camera. I began to take photographs to sort out my feelings about the summer that came before and the winter now well on its way.

Shari Altman

秋になると、また森へ通う日々がはじまります。そこは、彩度や陰影が増した世界。木々から葉が落ち、森が少し明るくなって、心を開いてくれる気がします。

ある日、近所の国立公園へ散歩に出かけ、観光客などがあまり来ないひっそりとした脇道でこの写真を撮りました。小川の淵に立って光が水面を踊る様子を眺めていると、空気は前日よりも明らかに冷たく感じられました。それは、私とカメラだけの、とてもひっそりとした時間。過ぎ去ったばかりの夏と、すぐそこまで迫る冬との狭間にある自分の気持ちと向き合うために、写真を撮りはじめました。

シャリ・アルトマン

Through the Lens

Shari is a photographer and blogger who lives in Vermont. She contributes a photo journal to this magazine.

シャリはヴァーモント在住のフォトグラファー、ブロガー。毎号 **amirisu** にフォト日記を寄稿しています。

$\mathcal{L}$ori's Notebook

Frame of Mind かぎ針で編むショール

"The pleasure we derive from journeys is perhaps dependent more on the mindset with which we travel than on the destination we travel to."

— Alain de Botton, The Art of Travel

I have been searching for the perfect take along knit for as long as I've been traveling. Planning for a project to bring can (and usually does!) take more time than packing clothes. I think I've finally found it, although it's not quite knitting – it's crochet.

Simple to learn, addictive, and virtually impossible to lose your place – it's a double crochet (treble in UK terms) triangle shawl.

Here is how to make it :

Materials: A size H-8 crochet hook. Approx. 600 yds of dk weight yarn, or 600 yds of fingering weight yarn to make approx. 45 x 22

「旅から得られる喜びは、どこへ向かうのかよりも、どんな心持ちで旅するのかに左右されるのではないだろうか。」

—アラン・ド ボトン著「旅する哲学—大人のための旅行術」より

旅行を頻繁にするようになってからというもの、ずっと旅に持っていくのにいい編みものはないかと試行錯誤してきました。洋服をパッキングするよりも、旅の編みものを選ぶほうが時間がかかることも。そしてついに見つけたのです。それは編みもの（英語では knit といえば棒針のこと）ではなくて、かぎ針だったのですが。

簡単に覚えられて病みつきになる、そしていつでもストップできる、長編みの三角ショール。

作りかたはこちら：

材料：5.0 号のかぎ針と DK または fingering の太さの毛糸を約 600 ヤード。ブロッキング前で約 114 x 56cm の三角ショールができます。

triangle (before blocking).

Row 1: Make a slip knot. Chain 4 – join to first stitch in slip stitch, chain up 3, double crochet into center ring. (make a cluster of 3)

Chain up 3 and turn your work.

Row 2: Work 2 more double crochets into the same stitch (it will be the first stitch).

Make 3 more double crochets into the LAST stitch (not the gap) chain up 3, turn your work.

Row 3: Work 2 more double crochets into the first stitch. Now begin working the cluster of 3 double crochets into each space.

Each row will continue this way, working 3 double crochets into the first and last stitch and 3 double crochets into each space. (do not yarn over between spaces).

Enjoy the journey and a peaceful Frame of Mind.

P.S. Crochet is also worry-free to those concerned about needles and airplanes. A hook will fit into a pencil case and can be easily carried on board.

段1：引き結びで1目作る。鎖を4目。最初の1目に引き抜き輪にする。鎖3目、輪に長編みを1目（3目のまとまりができる）。裏返す。

段2：立ち上がりの鎖3目。最初の目に長編み2目。最後の目に長編み3目。裏返す。

段3：立ち上がりの鎖3目。最初の目に長編み2目。前段の隙間に長編み3目を編み入れる。最後の目に長編み3目。裏返す。
これ以降、段3と同じ要領で編み続ける−最初と最後の目に3目ずつ、そしてその間の隙間にそれぞれ3目ずつを編む。

旅行の間、ゆったりとした気持ちで編みものを楽しんでくださいね。

追伸：飛行機に編み針を持ち込んでも大丈夫かどうかいつも気を揉むあなたには、かぎ針編みはオススメです。かぎ針はペンケースに簡単に収納でき、飛行機に持ち込みができますよ。

Photos courtesy of Lori Ann Graham

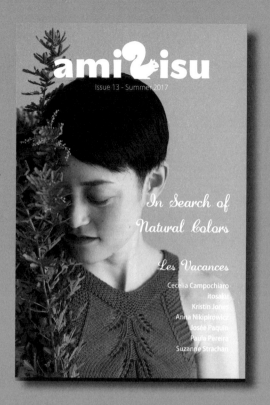

SUBSCRIBE!

amirisu is available for subscription! There will be three issues per year - 100 pages, printed on high quality paper.

Purchase three issues and receive a discount on cover price. Your copy will be delivered to you immediately after the release within the US and Japan (For the rest of the world, please allow a week for delivery).

For US details, please visit: https://amirisu-kurumi.myshopify.com

Non-US Countries: https://amirisu.myshopify.com/collections/amirisu-magazine

定期購読のお知らせ

amirisu の定期購読しませんか。カラー 100 頁、年 3 回の発行です。

3 号分の購読で雑誌と送料が割引に。日本国内には発売当日にお届けします。詳しくはこちらから：https://amirisu.myshopify.com

Bookish.

Animal Colorwork Bags
By Erika Tokai
From Seikodo Shinkousha

編み込み動物バッグ

東海えりか著

誠文堂新光社

This book was published last year in Japan, and I have been wanting to introduce it to the international knitting community ever since. For more than a decade, Erika Tokai has been a well-known hand-knit bag designer in Japan, and has been teaching widely. If you are an experienced knitter, your first glance at this book might make you think - "oh-oh, that looks hard." I agree, but the bags are irresistible and adorable. The book has a very detailed instructions on how to make one, with over 26 pages of full color photographs. There are 22 bag and 3 scarf designs included. My favorites are the red fox (on the cover), the lion, and the fawn, but it's so hard to pick one!

日本では昨年発売された本ですが、海外の皆さんに紹介したくて今回取り上げています。バッグのデザイナーとして長く活躍し、展示会やワークショップで人気の東海さん。比較的簡単に編めそうだった前回のお家の本と異なり、この動物バッグ、編みものが分かっている人なら見ただけで後ずさりしてしまいそうなインターシア。でも、表紙のバッグたちも、中に掲載されているバッグやマフラーも、どれも可愛くて作りたい気持ちが盛り上がること間違いなし。バッグに仕立てるまでのすべての工程が 26 ページに渡りカラー写真でとても丁寧に説明してあり、見ていると「これなら挑戦できるかも」と思えてきます。表紙の赤狐も、ライオンも、子鹿も可愛いし、まず最初に作る 1 つを選ぶのが一番難しい作業かもしれません。

Contributors

Fiona Alice

Fiona is a knitwear designer from Nova Scotia, Canada. In 2015, Fiona was living in London, UK, where published her first book with Pom Pom Press, Take Heart: A Transatlantic Knitting Journey. Currently, Fiona enjoys traveling and continues to gathering inspiration for new designs.

カナダのノヴァ・スコティア出身。2015年ロンドンに滞在し、Pom Pom Press より「Take Heart」を出版。現在は各地を旅しながらニットのデザインを行なっている。

Ravelry: FionaAlice
www.fionaalice.com
Instagram: @fiona_alice_

Mizuho Komiya

After studying fine art in college, Mizuho spent some years as a textile designer. She picked up knitting after giving birth to her first child, and has been knitting eversince. She regularly teaches at WALNUT Kyoto.

大学で油絵を学んだ後テキスタイルデザイナーを経て、出産の頃より編み物にハマる。以来自分らしいニット作品を作る事に情熱を傾けている。WALNUT KYOTO で週一回、4コマのレッスンを受け持っている。

Ravelry: Riku-fu
Instagram @rikufu.knit

Isabell Kraemer

Isabell is known for creating garments with seamless, top down construction. Heavily influenced by her beautiful natural environment, her aim is to design everyday items for modern knitters - casual garments with a little twist.

シームレスに編むトップダウンセーターのデザインで知られる。住まいの周りの美しい自然環境にインスピレーションを得ながら、現代的で普段使いできるニットをデザインしている。カジュアルで、一工夫あるものが好き。

Ravelry: lilalu
Instagram @lilalu72

Paula Pereira

Graduated in Marketing and Architecture, Paula worked as an entrepreneur before becoming a knitwear designer. She is particularly fond of mathematics and geometry which enables her to design garments with interesting constructions and always in a flattering shape.

マーケティングと建築を学んだ後、起業家としてファッションや美容分野で活躍。10年ほど前から編み物に目覚め、デザイナーとして活動を始めた。数学や幾何が特に大好きで、面白い構造や身体にあったフォルムを生みだすのに役に立っている。

Ravelry: PaulaPereira
Instagram: @paulapkl
peaceknitlove.com

Nele Redweik

Nele is a German expatriate dwelling in Portland, Ore. after living in Paris and Hawaii. Her background is in couture dressmaking and textile engineering, and nowadays she is the resident tailor and knitwear designer at Wildwood&Company. She also self-publishes and writes knitting patterns for yarn companies and magazines.

ドイツ出身、パリとハワイを経て、現在はオレゴン州ポートランド在住。大学ではドレスメーキングとテキスタイルエンジニアリングを学び、現在は Wildwood&Company でテイラー兼ニットデザイナーとして働く。

Ravelry: froschkoenigin89
Instagram: @nelekapparel

Camille Rosselle

Camille Rosselle is a stop motion filmmaker, a seamstress and a knitting designer. She works in Lyon (France) from where she creates her stories and garments. In her work she's looking for simple lines to keep things minimal.

フランスのリヨンで、ストップモーションの映画制作のかたわら、仕立てとニットデザインの仕事をする。ミニマルでシンプルなフォルムのデザインが好き。

Ravelry: Lerenard
Instagram: @camillerosselle
camillerosselle.wordpress.com

Nataliya Sinelshchikova

Born in Moscow, Nataliya moved to near Rotterdam a few years ago, and knitting helped her get adjusted to a quiet small-village life. She is a graphic designer and media artist by day and passionate knitter and crafter the rest of the time. She's passionate about color combinations, and loves minimalistic, yet effective designs.

モスクワ生まれ、数年前にロッテルダム近郊へ移住。大都会から小さい村への生活の変化を編み物が助けてくれた。日中はグラフィックデザイナーだが、普段から編み物やクラフトに夢中。色合わせ、そしてミニマルなデザインが好き。

Ravelry: FKSN
Instagram: @funky_knits

Ayano Tanaka

Ayano is a kniting addict, spending every spare time knitting or creating something from her ideas. Since seeing beautiful work in Estonia, she has been into knitting gloves.

隙間時間は編み、アイデアが浮かべば手を動かさずにはいられない編み物オタク。エストニアで素晴らしい手仕事を見て以来、最近は5本指手袋にはまっている。

Ravelry: ashika

Lori Ann Graham

Lori is a photographer, traveler, knitter and journal keeper from California. Her work appeared in publications including Lonely Planet's Traveller magazine, Photographer's Forum books, Shermans Travel, Making magazine and more. Her dream is to write a book someday.

写真家、旅行者、ニッターであり、日記を欠かさず付けているロリはカルフォルニアに暮らす。彼女の記事は、ロンリープラネットの旅行雑誌や、写真雑誌、最近刊行された Making などにも掲載、いつか本を出すのが夢。

Ravelry: lorix5
instagram : @loritimesfive

Maya Durham

Maya is eighteen and has just graduated high school. She's been making art her whole life, mostly preferring paint, ink and pencil. She's excited to have her work appear in **amirisu** magazine, which is a wonderful way to begin her artistic career. Although she doesn't knit often herself, Maya gets to appreciate and wear hand knits produced by her mother, knitwear designer Gudrun Johnston.

高校を卒業したばかりの18歳。油絵やペン画などが好きで、常にアートに没頭している。本誌に作品が掲載 (p.4-5) されてとても感激！編みものはたまにする程度だが、母親のグッドラン・ジョンソンの手編みセーターを着る幸運に恵まれている。

amirisu are:

Meri Tanaka　タナカメリ

Meri, the editor, creative and business development director, and co-rep of amirisu co., lives in the sacred city of Kyoto with a husband and a newborn boy. Past experience includes a+u magazine, management consulting and marketing.

2014 年夏より京都在住。編集・経営コンサル・マーケティング職を経て、amirisu co. で共同代表。編集、クリエティブ・ディレクション、マーチャンダイジング、企画等を担当。2017 年 3 月に出産し、1 児の母に。

Ravelry: sparklink02

Instagram: @Sparkle512

Tokuko Ochiai　オチアイトクコ

Tokuko is a knitwear designer and the co-representative of amirisu co., working non-stop to manage a yarn shop and knitting classes. She's finally used to all her finished projects being taken from her as shop samples. She lives in Nara.

ニットデザイナー、amirisu co. の共同代表として毛糸屋運営や教育に全力疾走する毎日。何を編んでも店のサンプルに取られるため、自分の編み物は全くできなくなったことにやっと慣れたところ。現在は奈良に居住し、相変わらず移動し続ける人生を送っている。

Ravelry: tokuko

Instagram: @knitwork

Yarn Shops 毛糸ショップ

Brick & mortar shops in Kyoto and Tokyo, as well as online shops.

US: amirisu-kurumi.myshopify.com

International incl. Japan: amirisu.myshopify.com

京都と表参道に実店舗があります。オンラインショップでの販売も行なっています。

amirisu.myshopify.com

Next Issue:
Winter 2017-18

Texture

To be released in January 2018

Atricle submissions related or unrelated to the topic is welcomed!

*For article contribution, please visit: www.amirisu.com/wp/contribute/ideas/

Next Submission Call

We are not planning a public call at this moment, but if things change, we will post on Facebook, Instagram and here: www. amirisu.com/wp/contribute/design/

Back when I was a student, I spent four weeks home-staying in the suburbs of London. School was in the morning only, and with my classmates from all over the world, I spent afternoons visiting markets, museums, and walking along the Thames, usually ending up at a pub. On one weekend, I even sang with a church choir for a wedding at a local 12th Century church with lovely stained glass windows (my host mother sort of tricked me without telling me the details.)

People may disagree, but my impression of London included how people used the color pink with abandon. From bright pink to pale pink, I loved how the color was used in dress shirts, ties, jackets, graphic designs and archi-tecture. There are many shades of pink, and I hope you will find ones that could work for you. We tend to go for darker colors such as gray, black and chocolate brown in autumn, but pink goes well with any of them and brightens up our skin tone.

Perhaps that is exactly why Londoners like pink - to brighten up their gloomy winter days.

Yes, winter - the season when we knitters flourish and party - and it's just around the corner. Are your needles ready?

Meri, **amirisu**

まだ学生のころ、ロンドンの郊外に4週間ほどホームステイをしました。語学学校は午前中だけだったので、世界中から集まっていたクラスメートたちとマーケットを歩き回ったり、美術館や博物館に行ったり、テムズ川を散歩したりとたくさんの時間を過ごし、そして大抵は最後はパブに行き着いていたものです。ある週末、12世紀に建てられた、当時のステンドグラスがそのまま残る教会に連れて行かれ、聖歌隊の1人として結婚式で歌ったこともありました（ホストマザーに事情を知らされず突然連れて行かれたのです）。結婚式に参列した人たちの驚いた顔が思い出されます。

あまり一般的な意見ではないかもしれませんが、ロンドンで過ごしたなかで印象深かったことのひとつは、ピンク色がそこかしこで効果的に使われていたこと。濃いピンクから淡いピンクまで、シャツやネクタイ、ジャケット、街の看板や建築の一部として、使われている様子が素敵でした。

ピンクと言っても様々な色味があります。この秋、皆さんに似合うとっておきのピンクが見つかりますように。秋冬になるとグレーや黒、チョコレートブラウンといった濃い色を選びがちですが、ピンクはいずれとも相性が良く、肌色を明るく見せてくれますよ。

もしかしたら、ロンドンでピンクがたくさん使われているのはまさに、暗い冬の日々を明るくするためかもしれません。

そう、冬。編みもの好きの私たちが水を得た魚のようにはしゃぎ回る季節はもうすぐそこです。準備はできていますか？

amirisu メリ

Casting Off...

Photo courtesy of Shari Altman

Patterns

Errata is available at below url.
パターンのエラーはこちらに記載します。
http://www.amirisu.com/shop/errata/

Pattern Questions
Please go to Ravelry amirisu group and post your
questions on a relevant thread.

本書に掲載するパターンのお問い合わせ
お問い合わせはRavelryのamirisuコミュニティボードよ
りお願いいたします。お電話でのお問い合わせではご
回答できかねますので、その旨予めご了承ください。
デザイナーと相談のうえ、ボード上で回答させていた
だきます。
http://www.ravelry.com/groups/amirisu

Gneiss by Fiona Alice

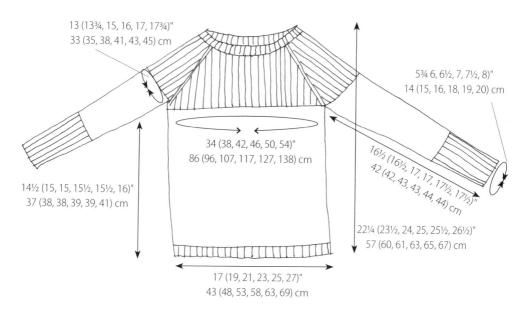

13 (13¾, 15, 16, 17, 17¾)"
33 (35, 38, 41, 43, 45) cm

5¾ 6, 6½, 7, 7½, 8)"
14 (15, 16, 18, 19, 20) cm

34 (38, 42, 46, 50, 54)"
86 (96, 107, 117, 127, 138) cm

14½ (15, 15, 15½, 15½, 16)"
37 (38, 38, 39, 39, 41) cm

16½ (16½, 17, 17, 17½, 17½)"
42 (42, 43, 43, 44, 44) cm

22¼ (23½, 24, 25, 25½, 26½)"
57 (60, 61, 63, 65, 67) cm

17 (19, 21, 23, 25, 27)"
43 (48, 53, 58, 63, 69) cm

Specifications

Yarn
DK weight yarn

(MC) Approximately 437 (503, 579, 666, 766, 880) yards, 400 (460, 529, 609, 700, 805) m

(CC) Approximately 563 (647, 745, 856, 984, 1131) yards, 515 (592, 681, 783, 900, 1035) m

La Bien Amiée Merino DK (100% superwash merino; 252 yards / 230 m, 115g)

Sample is shown in (MC) Ash 2 (2, 3, 3, 4, 4) skeins, (CC) Pom Pom 3 (3, 3, 4, 4, 5) skeins

Needles
A US 7 (4.5 mm) 24" / 60 cm circular needle

A US 6 (4 mm) straight or circular needle

A US 6 (4 mm) 16" / 40 cm circular needle

A set of US 6 (4 mm) double pointed needles (DPNs)

Or, needles required to obtain gauge

Gauge (after blocking)
20 stitches & 26 rows = 4"/10 cm in Reverse Stockinette Stitch with US 6 (4 mm) needles

Sizes
Finished chest measurements: XS (S, M, L, XL, XXL) = 34 (38, 42, 46, 50, 54)" / 87 (97, 107, 117, 127, 137) cm

The sample was knit in size S with 6" / 15 cm positive ease.

Tools
Stitch markers (4), tapestry needle, waste yarn

Stitch Guide
Work in pattern: Knit the knit stitches, purl the purl stitches, SM as you work across the row

Skill Level
●●●●○

Notes
This sweater begins as a top down design. Once the piece is ready to be divided for the sleeves, the front and back are then worked separately to allow for the two-color Intarsia pattern on the back. After the front and back are both finished, the sweater's side seams are sewn together and then the sleeves are picked up and worked in the round. If using hand dyed yarn for this design, it is recommended to alternate between two balls at once to create a fabric with even color distribution.

Instruction

Body

With Long-Tail Cast-On method in MC yarn, CO 53 (59, 63, 67, 73, 77) sts using larger needle.

Set-up Row (WS) : P2, PM, P2, [K1, P1] 3 (4, 4, 4, 4, 3) times, P1, PM, P2, [K1, P1] 14 (15, 17, 19, 22, 26) times, P1, PM, P2, [K1, P1] 3 (4, 4, 4, 4, 3) times, P1, PM, P2.

Row 1: Work in pattern to 1 st before M, * M1PR, K1, SM, K1, M1PL, [K1, P1] to 2 sts before M, K1; repeat from * twice, M1PR, K1, SM, K1, M1PL, work in pattern to end. 8 sts increased. Total 61 (67, 71, 75, 81, 85) sts.

Row 2: Work in pattern.

Row 3: Work in pattern to 1 st before M, * M1R, K1, SM, K1, M1L, P1, [K1, P1] to 1 st before M; repeat from * twice, M1R, K1, SM, K1, M1L, work in pattern to end. 8 sts increased. Total 69 (75, 79, 83, 89, 93) sts.

Row 4: Same as Row 2.

Repeat Rows 1 - 4 twice.

Work Rows 1 & 2 again.

Row 15: Kfb, work in pattern to 1 st before M, * M1R, K1, SM, K1, M1L, P1, [K1, P1] to 1 st before M; repeat from * twice, M1R, K1, SM, K1, M1L, work in pattern to last st, Kfb. 10 sts increased. Total 119 (125, 129, 133, 139, 143) sts.

Row 16: K1, P1, work in pattern to last 2 sts, P1, K1.

Row 17: Kfb, work in pattern to 1 st before M, * M1PR, K1, SM, K1, M1PL, [K1, P1] to 2 sts before M, K1; repeat from * twice, M1PR, K1, SM, K1, M1PL, work in pattern to last sts, Kfb. 10 sts increased. Total 129 (135, 139, 143, 149, 153) sts.

Row 18: P1, K1, work in pattern to last 2 sts, K1, P1.

Row 19: Kfb, work in pattern to 1 st before M, * M1R, K1, SM, K1, M1L, P1, [K1, P1] to 1 st before M; repeat from * twice, M1R, K1, SM, K1, M1L, work in pattern to last st, Kfb, CO 21 (23, 27, 31, 37, 45) with Backward Loop Cast On method, PM and join to work in the round. This last marker will now be the BOR. Total 160 (168, 176, 184, 196, 208) sts.

Rnd 20: P1, work in pattern to end, working [P1, K1] or [K1, P1] into the CO sts.

Rnd 21: Work in pattern to 1 st before M, * M1PR, K1, SM, K1, M1PL, [K1, P1] to 2 sts before M; repeat from * 3 times, work in pattern to end. 8 sts increased. Total 168 (176, 184, 192, 204, 216) sts.

Rnd 22: Work in pattern to end.

Rnd 23: Work in pattern to 1 st before M, * M1R, K1, SM, K1, M1L, P1, [K1, P1] to 1 st before M; repeat from * 3 times, work in pattern to end. 8 sts increased. Total 176 (184, 192, 200, 212, 224) sts.

Rnd 24: Work in pattern to end.

Repeat Rnds 21 - 24, until there are 272 (296, 320, 344, 372, 400) sts. Work Rnds 21 & 22 again. Total 280 (304, 328, 352, 380, 408) sts.

Work in pattern until piece measures 7¾ (8½, 9, 9½, 10, 10½)" / 20 (22, 23, 24, 25, 27) cm from CO of back.

Work in pattern to 1st M, break MC, leave a tail to weave in later. TW and join CC to begin Front. Separate sleeves from Back and put them on waste yarn. The Back can be placed on waste yarn, as well. 59 (65, 69, 73, 77, 79) sts for each sleeve and 81 (87, 95, 103, 113, 125) sts for Back.

Front

Set Up Row (WS): CO 2 (4, 5, 6, 6, 5) sts with smaller needle and Backward Loop Cast On method in CC, work in pattern across Front, CO 2 (4, 5, 6, 6, 5) sts with Backward Loop Cast On method, turn work. Total 85 (95, 105, 115, 125, 135) sts.

Row 1 (RS): P to end.

Row 2 (WS): K to end.

Work in Reverse Stockinette Stitch until side seam measures 13½ (14, 14, 14½, 14½, 15)" / 34 (36, 36, 37, 37, 38) cm, ending with a RS row. With WS facing, purl to end.

Next Row (RS): [K1, P1] to last st, K1.

Next Row (WS): [P1, K1] to last st, P1.

Work in 1x1 ribbing for 1" / 2.5 cm, BO in pattern.

Back

The Back section is worked in Intarsia. Two balls of CC and one ball of MC will be needed. It is important to twist the yarns together when changing colors to stop a hole from forming.

Set Up Row (WS): With the first ball of CC, CO 2 (4, 5, 6, 5) sts on to larger needle using the Backward Loop Cast On method, rejoin MC and work in pattern across Back, with the second ball of CC, CO 2 (4, 5, 6, 6, 5) sts using the Backward Loop Cast On method. Total 85 (95, 105, 115, 125, 135) sts.

Row 1 (RS): With CC [P across CC sts, K1], with MC [work in pattern to 1 sts before CC sts], with CC [K1, P to end].

Row 2 (WS): With CC [K across CC sts, P1], with MC [work in pattern to 1 st before CC sts], with CC [P1, K to end].

Repeat Rows 1 & 2 of Intarsia section until one MC st remains in the center.

Row 3 (RS): Change to US 6 / 4 mm needle and with CC, P to center st, K1, P to end. Break MC and other CC, leaving a tail to weave in later. Continue with just one ball of CC from this point.

Row 4 (WS): Knit to end.

Work in Reverse Stockinette Stitch until side seam measures 13½ (14, 14, 14½, 14½, 15)" / 34 (36, 36, 37, 37, 38) cm, ending with a RS row. With WS facing, purl to end.

Next Row (RS): [K1, P1] to last st, K1.

Next Row (WS): [P1, K1] to last st, P1.

Work in 1x1 ribbing for 1" / 2.5 cm, BO in pattern.

The side seams will need to be finished before moving onto the sleeves. Use Mattress Stitch for Reverse Stockinette Stitch to seam sides.

Sleeves

With smaller needle, start at underarm and pick up 2 (4, 5, 6, 6, 5) sts from the previous CO sts left of seam, place Sleeve sts onto needle, pick up another 2 (4, 5, 6, 6, 5) sts from CO sts right of seam. Join for working in the round, PM here to indicate BOR. Total 63 (73, 79, 85, 89, 89) sts.

Set Up Rnd: With CC, P2tog 0 (2, 2, 3, 2, 0) times, P2 (0, 1, 0, 2, 5), work in pattern to last 2 (4, 5, 6, 6, 5) sts, P2 (0, 1, 0, 2, 5), P2tog 0 (2, 2, 3, 2, 0) times. Total 63 (69, 75, 79, 85, 89) sts.

Work in Reverse Stockinette Stitch until sleeve measures 2¾ (2, 1¾, 1, 1½, 1½)" / 7 (5, 4, 3, 4, 4) cm.

Rnd 1: P1, SSP, P to last 3 sts, P2tog, P1. 2 sts decreased.

Rnds 2 - 6: Purl to end.

Repeat Rnds 1 - 6 till 51 (53, 57, 61, 65, 69) sts remain.

Next Rnd: K1, K2tog, K to end. 1 st decreased. Total 50 (52, 56, 60, 64, 68) sts.

Change to MC, [K1, P1] to end.

Continue to work in 1x1 ribbing until sleeve measures 16½ (16½, 17, 17, 17½, 17½)" / 42 (42, 43, 43, 44, 44) cm, BO in pattern.

Repeat for second Sleeve.

Neckband

With smaller needle and MC, start at center Back and pick up 96 (104, 112, 120, 128, 136) sts around the neck opening for neckband. The exact number is not critical, just as long as there is an even number. PM to indicate BOR.

Rnd 1: [K1, P1] to end.

Continue to work in 1 x 1 ribbing until piece measures 2" / 5 cm from neckline.

Break yarn, leaving a tail approximately 2½-3 times as long as the circumference of your neckband.

Turn garment inside-out and fold neckband toward the WS.

Thread tail end onto a tapestry needle. Using Whip Stitch, and continuing in the same direction as you would for working another round, tack live neckband stitches to inside of garment as follows:

Step 1: Insert tapestry needle into next stitch on needle, letting it slip off the needle.

Step 2: Insert tapestry needle into corresponding row of pick-up edge of neckband, pulling yarn through to close. Note: Do not pull too tightly, as this edge needs to remain elastic.

Repeat Steps 1 & 2 around neckband until all stitches have been secured.

Weave in all ends invisibly on the WS of garment.

Finishing

Weave in end, soak and gently block to measurements.

詳細情報

Yarn

DK weight yarn

(MC) 約437 (503, 579, 666, 766, 880) yards, 400 (460, 529, 609, 700, 805) m

(CC) 約563 (647, 745, 856, 984, 1131) yards, 515 (592, 681, 783, 900, 1035) m

La Bien Amiée Merino DK (100% superwash merino; 252 yards / 230 m, 115g)

サンプルは(MC) Ash 2 (2, 3, 3, 4, 4)カセ, (CC) Pom Pom 3 (3, 3, 4, 4, 5) カセ

Needles

US 7 (4.5 mm), 24" / 60 cmの輪針

1 × US 6 (4 mm)の2本棒針, もしくは輪針

1 × US 6 (4 mm), 16" / 40 cmの輪針

1 × US 6 (4 mm), 短針セット

または, ゲージが取れる太さの針

Gauge (ブロッキング後)

US 6 (4 mm)の針を使用し, 裏メリヤス編みで20目 & 26段 = 10 cm

Sizes

出来上がり寸法: 胸囲XS (S, M, L, XL, XXL) = 87 (97, 107, 117, 127, 137) cm

モデルはSサイズを着用し, 余裕として+15 cm.

Tools

目数マーカー (4), 綴じ針, 別糸

Stitch Guide

パターン通りに編む: KはKで編み, PはPで編み, 途中でMがあった場合はSMしながら編む.

Skill Level

Note

トップダウンで編むセーター. 袖を分けるまで編んだら, 後ろ身頃と前身頃を別々に分け, 後ろ身頃は2色を使ってインターシアの技法で編む. 両身頃を編み終わった後, 脇を綴じはぎし, 袖目を拾い, 袖を輪で編む. 手染め糸を使う場合, 編地の色を均等に保つため, 糸玉を二つ用い, 毎段交互にストライプを編むように編むことをお勧めする.

編みかた

身頃

MCと太い方の針を用い, 指で掛ける作り目で, CO 53 (59, 63, 67, 73, 77)目.

セットアップ段 (WS) : P2, PM, P2, [K1, P1] を3 (4, 4, 4, 4, 3) 回繰り返す, P1, PM, P2, [K1, P1] を 14 (15, 17, 19, 22, 26)回繰り返す, P1, PM, P2, [K1, P1]を 3 (4, 4, 4, 4, 3)回繰り返す, P1, PM, P2.

段 1: Mの1目前までパターン通り編む, * M1PR, K1, SM, K1, M1PL, [K1, P1]をMの2目前まで繰り返す, K1; *からを2回繰り返す, M1PR, K1, SM, K1, M1PL, 最後までパターン通り編む. 8目増目. 計61 (67, 71, 75, 81, 85)目.

段 2: パターン通り編む.

段 3: Mの1目前までパターン通り編む, * M1R, K1, SM, K1, M1L, P1, [K1, P1] をMの1目前まで繰り返す; *からを2回繰り返す, M1R, K1, SM, K1, M1L, 最後までパターン通り編む . 8 目増目. 計69 (75, 79, 83, 89, 93)目.

段 4: 段 2と同様に編む.

段1 – 4を2回編む.

段 1 & 2を編む.

段 15: Kfb, Mの1目前までパターン通りに編む, * M1R, K1, SM, K1, M1L, P1, [K1, P1]を Mの1目前まで繰り返す; *からを2回繰り返す, M1R, K1, SM, K1, M1L, 最後の1目前までパターン通り編む, Kfb. 10 目増目. 計119 (125, 129, 133, 139, 143)目.

段 16: K1, P1, 最後の2目前までパターン通り編む, P1, K1.

段 17: Kfb, Mの1目前までパターン通りに編む, * M1PR, K1, SM, K1, M1PL, [K1, P1] をMの2目前まで繰り返す, K1; *からを2回繰り返す, M1PR, K1, SM, K1, M1PL, 最後の1目までパターン通り編む , Kfb. 10 目増目. 計129 (135, 139, 143, 149, 153)目 .

段 18: P1, K1, 最後の2目前までパターン通り編む, K1, P1.

段 19: Kfb, Mの1目前までパターン通りに編む, * M1R, K1, SM, K1, M1L, P1, [K1, P1]を Mの1目前まで繰り返す; *からを2回繰り返す, M1R, K1, SM, K1, M1L, 最後の1目前までパターン通り編む, Kfb, 巻き増し目でCO 21 (23, 27, 31, 37, 45), BORM(編み始めのM)を入れ輪にする. 計160 (168, 176, 184, 196, 208)目.

周 20: P1, COの目も [P1, K1] または [K1, P1] を編みながら, パターン通り最後まで編む.

周 21: Mの1目前までパターン通りに編む, * M1PR, K1, SM, K1, M1PL, [K1, P1] をMの2目前まで繰り返す; *からを 3 回繰り返す, 最後までパターン通り編む. 8 目増目. 計168 (176, 184, 192, 204, 216)目 .

周 22: 最後までパターン通り編む.

周 23: Mの1目前までパターン通りに編む, * M1R, K1, SM, K1, M1L, P1, [K1, P1] をMの1目前まで繰り返す; *からを 3 回繰り返す, 最後までパターン通り編む. 8 目増目. 計176 (184, 192, 200, 212, 224)目 .

周 24: 最後までパターン通り編む.

周 21 – 24を目数が272 (296, 320, 344, 372, 400)目になるまで繰り返す.

周 21 & 22 をもう一度編む. 計280 (304, 328, 352, 380, 408)目 .

後ろ身頃の作り目からの長さが20 (22, 23, 24, 25, 27) cmになるまでパターン通り編む.

1番目のMまでパターン通り編む, 糸始末できるぐらいの長さを残してMCの糸を切る. 編地を返し, CCの糸を付け前身頃を始める. 後ろ身頃から袖目を別糸に休め, 同じように後ろ身頃も別糸に休める. 各袖目として59 (65, 69, 73, 77, 79)目, 後ろ身頃として81 (87, 95, 103, 113, 125)目.

前身頃

セットアップ段 (WS): CCと細い方の針を用い, 巻き増し目でCO 2 (4, 5, 6, 6, 5), 前身頃をパターン通り編む , 巻き増し目でCO 2 (4, 5, 6, 6, 5)目, 編地を返す. 計85 (95, 105, 115, 125, 135)目 .

段 1 (RS): 最後までP.

段 2 (WS): 最後までK.

脇の綴じる部分が34 (36, 36, 37, 37, 38) cmになるまで裏メリヤス編みを続ける, 最後はRS段.

WSを見て, Pで1 段編む.

次の段 (RS): [K1, P1] を最後の1目まで繰り返す, K1.

次の段 (WS): [P1, K1] を最後の1目まで繰り返す, P1.

この1目ゴム編みを2.5 cm編み, パターン通り編みながらBO.

後ろ身頃

後ろ身頃部分はインターシア(縦に糸を渡す編み込みの技法)を使う. 二つのCCの糸玉と一つのMCの糸玉が必要. 糸替えをする際は必ず, 双方の糸をからめて, 穴が開くことを防ぐようにする.

セットアップ段 (WS): 太い方の針とCCの一つ目の糸玉を用い, 巻き増し目でCO 2 (4, 5, 6, 6, 5), MCを用い後ろ身頃をパターン通り編む, CCの二つ目の糸玉を用い, 巻き増し目でCO 2 (4, 5, 6, 6, 5). 計85 (95, 105, 115, 125, 135)目 .

段 1 (RS): CCで [CC色の目をP, K1], MCで [CC色の1目前までパターン通り編む], CCで [K1, 最後までP].

段 2 (WS): CCで [CC 色の目をK, P1], MCで [CC色の1目前までパターン通り編む], CCで [P1, 最後までK].

段1 & 2 のインターシアをMCが中央1目に残るまで繰り返す.

段 3 (RS): 4 mmの針に替えCCで中央の目を P , K1, 最後までP. MCともう一つのCCの糸玉の糸を糸始末できるぐらいの長さを残して切る. 残ったCCの糸玉で編んでいく.

段 4 (WS): 最後までK.

脇の綴じる部分が34 (36, 36, 37, 37, 38) cmになるまで, 裏メリヤス編みを続ける, 最後はRS段.

WSを見て, Pで1 段編む.

次の段 (RS): [K1, P1] を最後の1目前まで繰り返す, K1.

次の段 (WS): [P1, K1] を最後の1目前まで繰り返す, P1.

この1目ゴム編みを2.5 cm編み, パターン通り編みながらBO.

袖を編む前に, 脇をすくいとじで綴じる.

袖

細い方の針を用い, 脇下中央から始める. 糸を付けず左側のCO部分から2 (4, 5, 6, 6, 5)目を拾い, 休めていた袖目を針に移し, 脇下の右側のCO部分から2 (4, 5, 6, 6, 5)目拾う. BORMを入れ輪にする. 計63 (73, 79, 85, 89, 89)目 .

セットアップ周: CCを付け, P2togを 0 (2, 2, 3, 2, 0) 回繰り返す, P2 (0, 1, 0, 2, 5), 最後の2 (4, 5, 6, 6, 5)目前までパターン通り編む, P2 (0, 1, 0, 2, 5), P2togを 0 (2, 2, 3, 2, 0) 回繰り返す. 計63 (69, 75, 79, 85, 89)目 .

袖の長さが7 (5, 4, 3, 4, 4) cmになるまで裏メリヤス編みを続ける.

周 1: P1, SSP, 最後の3目前までP, P2tog, P1. 2目減目.

周 2 - 6: 最後までP.

周 1 – 6を残り51 (53, 57, 61, 65, 69)目になるまで繰り返す.

次の周: K1, K2tog, 最後までK. 1目減目. 計50 (52, 56, 60, 64, 68)目.

MCに替え, [K1, P1]を最後まで繰り返す.

この1目ゴム編みを袖の長さが42 (42, 43, 43, 44, 44) cmになるまで編み, パターン通り編みながらBO.

2本目も同じように編む.

首回り

細い方の針とMCを用い, 後ろ身頃中心からスタート. 96 (104, 112, 120, 128, 136)目, 首周りから拾う. その際, この目数通りに正確に拾う必要はないが, 偶数にする必要はある. 編み始めにBORMを入れる.

周 1: [K1, P1] を最後まで編む.

この1目ゴム編みを5 cm編む.

襟ぐりの周囲の約2.5-3倍の長さを残して糸を切る.

編み地を裏返し, 襟ぐりを裏側に折り返す. 端糸を綴じ針に通す.

編む方向と同じ向きにまつり縫いで, 目を襟ぐりの裏側に次のように留める:

ステップ1: 綴じ針を次の目に通し, その目を針から落とす.

ステップ2: 綴じ針を襟ぐりの拾い目部に通し, 最後まで引き抜く.

Note: 伸縮性を保つため, 強く引っ張り過ぎないこと.

ステップ1 & 2を1周繰り返す.

裏側で目立たないように端糸をすべて始末する.

仕上げ

糸始末をし, 寸法通りになるようブロッキングする.

Devon by Paula Pereira

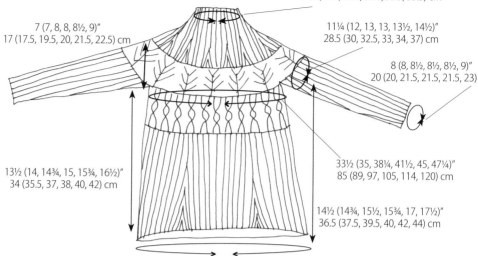

19½ (20¾, 20¾, 20¾, 22, 22)"
49.5 (52.5, 52.5, 52.5, 55.5, 55.5) cm

7 (7, 8, 8, 8½, 9)"
17 (17.5, 19.5, 20, 21.5, 22.5) cm

11¼ (12, 13, 13, 13½, 14½)"
28.5 (30, 32.5, 33, 34, 37) cm

8 (8, 8½, 8½, 8½, 9)"
20 (20, 21.5, 21.5, 21.5, 23) cm

13½ (14, 14¾, 15, 15¾, 16½)"
34 (35.5, 37, 38, 40, 42) cm

33½ (35, 38¼, 41½, 45, 47¼)"
85 (89, 97, 105, 114, 120) cm

14½ (14¾, 15½, 15¾, 17, 17½)"
36.5 (37.5, 39.5, 40, 42, 44) cm

37 (39, 41¾, 45, 48½, 51)" / 94 (98.5, 106, 114, 123, 129.5) cm

Specifications

Yarn
Worsted weight yarn

Approximately 1320 (1390, 1580, 1700, 1920, 2040) yards / 1210 (1275, 1450, 1560, 1760, 1870) m

10 (10, 12, 13, 14, 15) skeins of Brooklyn Tweed Shelter (100 % American Targhee-Columbia Wool; 140 yards / 50g)

Sample is shown in Camper

Needles
A US 7 (4.5 mm) 32" / 80 cm (or longer) circular needle

A US 7 (4.5 mm) 16" / 40 cm circular needle

A US 4 (3.5 mm) 16" / 40 cm circular needle

A set of US 7 (4.5 mm) double pointed needles (DPNs)

A set of US 4 (3.5 mm) double pointed needles (DPNs)

Or, needles required to obtain gauge

Gauge (after blocking)
26 stitches & 31 rows = 4" / 10 cm in 1 X 1 Twisted Rib with US 7 (4.5 mm) needle

Sizes
Finished chest measurements: XS (S, M, L, XL, XXL) = 34 (36, 38½, 42, 46, 48½)" / 86 (91, 98, 107, 117, 123) cm

The sample was knit in size S with 3½" / 9 cm positive ease.

Tools
Stitch markers, tapestry needle, cable needle, waste yarn

Stitch Guide
Special Stitch (SS): (over 3 sts) leaving on the LH needle,

pass 3rd stitch over 2nd and 1st stitches; pass 2nd stitch over 1st stitch. Then, (K1, YO, K1) on this st.

1 x 1 Twisted Rib (in the round):
Rnd 1: *(K1tbl, P1) or *(P1, K1tbl), repeat * to end.

Repeat round 1.

1 x 1 Twisted Rib (flat):
Row 1: *(K1tbl, P1) or *(P1, K1tbl), repeat * to end.

Row 2: *(K1, P1tbl) or * (P1tbl, K1), repeat * to end.

Repeat rows 1 and 2.

1/1/1 LPT: Slip 1 st to CN and hold in front, slip next st to second CN and hold in back, K1 tbl, P1 from back CN, K1 tbl from front CN.

1/1/1 RPT: Slip 2 sts to CN and hold in back, K1 tbl, slip 1 st from CN to left needle and move CN to front, P1, K1 tbl from CN.

Skill Level

Notes
The sweater is worked seamlessly from the top down and in the round. The CO is the edge of the neck band. After the yoke, separate body and place sleeve stitches on waste yarn or a stitch holder. The sleeves are also worked in the round after you pick up the stitches that are on hold, and can be knitted using either the Magic Loop method or DPNs.

Back neck shaping and the rounded back hem are knit with Short Rows, over the 1 x 1 Twisted Ribbing.

The Rib Cast-On method and the Tubular Bind-Off method provide the rounded and continuous look at the edges of the sweater.

A stitch marker is placed in the middle of the back neck.

Instruction

Yoke

Neckband

With smaller needle and Long-Tail Tubular Cast-On method, CO 128 (136, 136, 136, 144, 144) sts. PM and join in the round.

Work 2 rounds in 1 x 1 Twisted Rib (K1tbl, P).

Sizes XS (S, M, L, XL)

Change to larger needles and work 18 rounds in 1 x 1 Twisted Rib. Total 128 (136, 136, 136,144) sts.

Size XXL only

Change to larger needles and work 5 rounds in 1 x 1 Twisted Rib.

Increase Rnd: (K1tbl, P1) 14 times, (K1tbl, P1, K1tbl) in one st, (P1, K1tbl) 7 times, (P1, K1tbl, P1) in one st, (K1tbl, P1) 28 times, (K1tbl, P1, K1tbl) in one st, (P1, K1tbl) 7 times, (P1, K1tbl, P1) in one st, (K1tbl, P1) 14 times. Total 152 sts.

Work 5 rounds in 1 x 1 Twisted Rib.

Increase Rnd: (K1tbl, P1) 14 times, K1tbl, (P1, K1tbl, P1) in one st, (K1tbl, P1) 8 times, (K1tbl, P1, K1tbl) in one st, (P1, K1tbl) 29 times, (P1, K1tbl, P1) in one st, (K1tbl, P1) 8 times, (K1tbl, P1, K1tbl) in one st, (P1, K1tbl) 14 times, P1. Total 160 sts.

Work 6 rounds in 1 x 1 Twisted Rib.

Total 128 (136, 136, 136, 144, 160) sts.

Back Neck Shaping

Instead of "wraps", work the YOs with the next stitches together in pattern, as they show up.

Short Row 1: (K1tbl, P1) 4 times, TW.

Short Row 2: YO, (K1, P1tbl) 8 times, TW.

Short Row 3 to 10: YO, work as established to 8 sts after last turn and TW.

Short Row 11 to 14: YO, work as established to 8 (10, 10, 10, 12, 12) sts after last turn and TW.

Short Row 15: YO, work as established to M. At next round, purl the last YO and one stitch before the YO together.

Yoke

Set-up Rnd: *(K1tbl, P1) 4 times, PM, repeat from * to end.

Total 128 (136, 136, 136, 144, 160) sts.

Sizes XS and S (Chart 1)

Work Rnds 1 to 46 of Chart 1. Total 288 (306) sts.

Only Size S

Repeat Rnd 46 more 4 times. Total 50 rounds.

Sizes M, L, XL and XXL (Chart 2)

Work Rnds 1 to 56 of Chart 2.

Total 340 (340, 360, 400) sts.

Repeat Rnd 56 more 0 (2, 6, 10) times. Total 56 (58, 62, 66) rounds.

Rnd 47 (51, 57, 59, 63, 67): P all sts.

Sizes XS and M

Rnd 48 (58): K all sts.

Sizes S, L, XL and XXL

Increase Rnd 52 (60, 64, 68): P all sts, increase evenly 2 (8, 16, 8) sts with Pfb.

Total 288 (308, 340, 348, 376, 408) sts.

Rnd 49 (53, 59, 61, 65, 69): *(K2tog tbl, YO), repeat * to end.

Rnd 50 (54, 60, 62, 66, 70): *(P1, P1tbl) repeat * to end.

Separate Body and Sleeves

Set-up Rnd 51 (55, 61, 63, 67, 71): P45 (48, 53, 56, 62, 66) sts, transfer 54 (58, 64, 62, 64, 72) sts onto waste yarn, CO 20 (20, 20, 24, 24, 24) sts with Backward Loop Cast-On method, P90 (96, 106, 112, 124, 132) sts, transfer 54 (58, 64, 62, 64, 72) sts onto waste yarn, CO 20 (20, 20, 24, 24, 24) sts with Backward Loop Cast-On method, P45 (48, 53, 56, 62, 66) sts. Total 220 (232, 252, 272, 296, 312) sts.

Work 5 rounds in 1 x 1 Twisted Rib.

Sizes XS and S

Rnd 57 (61): P1, *(SS, P1) repeat *to end.

Sizes M, L, XL and XXL

Rnd 67 (69,73,77): *(SS, P1) repeat *to end.

All Sizes

Work 5 rounds in 1 x 1 Twisted Rib.

Sizes XS and S

Rnd 63 (67): P1, *(SS, P1) repeat *to end.

Sizes M, L, XL and XXL

Rnd 73 (75,79,83): *(SS, P1) repeat *to end

All Sizes

Work 5 rounds in 1 x 1 Twisted Rib.

Rnd 69 (73, 79, 81, 85, 89) and 70 (74, 80, 82, 86, 90): P all sts.

Rnd 71 (75, 81, 83, 87, 91): *(K2tog tbl, YO), repeat * to end.

Rnd 72 (76, 82, 84, 88, 92) and 73 (77, 83, 85, 89, 93): P all sts.

Sizes XS and S

Starting with P, work 7 (7) rounds in 1 x 1 Twisted Rib.

Sizes M, L, XL and XXL

Starting with K1tbl, work 7 (7, 9, 11) rounds in 1 x 1 Twisted Rib.

Body Increases

Sizes XS and S

Rnd 81 (85): (P1, K1tbl) 10 (11) times, (P1, K1tbl, P1) in one st, (K1tbl, P1) 34 (35) times, (K1tbl, P1, K1tbl) in one st, (P1, K1tbl) 20 (22) times, (P1, K1tbl, P1) in one st. (K1tbl, P1) 34 (35) times, (K1tbl, P1, K1tbl) in one st, (P1, K1tbl) 10 (11) times. Total 228 (240) sts.

Sizes M, L, XL and XXL

Rnd 91 (93, 99, 105): (K1tbl, P1) 11 (12, 12, 13) times, (K1tbl, P1, K1tbl) in one st, (P1, K1tbl) 40 (43, 49, 51) times, (P1, K1tbl, P1) in one st, (K1tbl, P1) 22 (24, 24, 26) times, (K1tbl, P1, K1tbl) in one st, (P1, K1tbl) 40 (43, 49, 51) times, (P1, K1tbl, P1) in one st, (K1tbl, P1) 11 (12, 12, 13) times. Total 260 (280, 304, 320) sts.

All Sizes

Work as established for 9 rounds in 1 x 1 Twisted Rib.

Sizes XS and S

Rnd 91 (95): (P1, K1tbl) 10 (11) times, P1, (K1tbl, P1, K1tbl) in one st, (P1, K1tbl) 35 (36) times, (P1, K1tbl, P1) in one st, (K1tbl, P1) 21 (23) times, (K1tbl, P1, K1tbl) in one st, (P1, K1tbl) 35 (36) times, (P1, K1tbl, P1) in one st, (K1tbl, P1) 10 (11) times, K1tbl. Total 236 (248) sts.

Sizes M, L, XL and XXL

Rnd 101 (103, 109, 115): (K1tbl, P1) 11 (12, 12, 13) times, K1tbl, (P1, K1tbl, P1) in one st, (K1tbl, P1) 41 (44, 50, 52) times, (K1tbl, P1, K1tbl) in one st, (P1, K1tbl) 23 (25, 25, 27) times, (P1, K1tbl, P1) in one st, (K1tbl, P1) 41 (44, 50, 52) times, (K1tbl, P1, K1tbl) in one st, (P1, K1tbl) 11 (12, 12, 13) times, P1. Total 268 (288, 312, 328) sts.

All Sizes

Work as established for 13 rounds in 1 x 1 Twisted Rib.

Sizes XS and S

Rnd 105 (109): (P1, K1tbl) 11 (12) times, (P1, K1tbl, P1) in one st, (K1tbl, P1) 36 (37) times, (K1tbl, P1, K1tbl) in one st, (P1, K1tbl) 22 (24) times, (P1, K1tbl, P1) in one st, (K1tbl, P1) 36 (37) times, (K1tbl, P1, K1tbl) in one st, (P1, K1tbl) 11 (12) times. Total 244 (256) sts.

Sizes M, L, XL and XXL

Rnd 115 (117, 123, 129): (K1tbl, P1) 12 (13, 13, 14) times, (K1tbl, P1, K1tbl) in one st, (P1, K1tbl) 42 (45, 51, 53) times, (P1, K1tbl, P1) in one st, (K1tbl, P1) 24 (26, 26, 28) times, (K1tbl, P1, K1tbl) in one st, (P1, K1tbl) 42 (45, 51, 53) times, (P1, K1tbl, P1) in one st, (K1tbl, P1) 12 (13, 13, 14) times. Total 276 (296, 320, 336) sts.

All Sizes

Work as established in 1 x 1 Twisted Rib until piece measures 15 (15, 16, 16, 17, 17)" / 38 (38, 41, 41, 43, 43) cm from underarm Cast-On.

Back Hem

Sizes XS and S

Short Row 1: (P1, K1tbl) 41 (44) times, W&T.

Short Row 2: (P1tbl, K1) 82 (88) times, W&T.

Short Row 3 and 4: Work as established in 1 x 1 rib until 3 sts before last wrapped st, W&T.

Short Row 5 and 6: Work as established in 1 x 1 rib until 2 sts before last wrapped st, W&T.

Short Row 7: Work the wraps as you find them and work as established in 1 x 1 rib until M.

Sizes M, L, XL and XXL

Short Row 1: (K1tbl, P1) 47 (51, 56, 59) times, W&T.

Short Row 2: (K1, P1tbl) 94 (102, 112, 118) times, W&T.

Short Row 3 and 4: Work as established in 1 x 1 rib until 3 sts before last wrapped st, W&T.

Short Row 5 and 6: Work as established in 1 x 1 rib until 2 sts before last wrapped st, W&T.

Short Row 7: Work the wraps as you find them and work as established in 1 x 1 rib until M.

All Sizes

Work as established for 2 rounds in 1 x 1 Twisted Rib. Using the Tubular Bind-Off method, BO all sts in pattern.

Sleeves

Place 54 (58, 64, 62, 64, 72) sts of one sleeve on US 7 (4.5mm) DPNs or smaller needles. Attach yarn and starting with a knit st at the center of the underarm, pick up and knit 10 (10, 10, 12, 12, 12) sts, work in pattern across sleeve sts, pick up and knit 10 (10, 10, 12, 12, 12) sts. PM and join for working in the round. Total 74 (78, 84, 86, 88, 96) sts.

Work 8 (7, 6, 6, 6, 5) rounds in 1 x 1 Twisted Rib (K1tbl, P1).

Decrease Rnd: K1tbl, K2tog, work in 1 x 1 Twisted Rib until last 2 sts before M, SSK. 2 sts decrease – Total 72 (76, 82, 84, 86, 94) sts.

Repeat last 9 (8, 7, 7, 7, 6) rounds more 10 (12, 13, 14, 15, 17) times. Total 52 (52, 56, 56, 56, 60) sts.

Work in 1 x 1 Twisted Rib 26 (24, 34, 28, 22, 26) rounds more, or until ½" / 1 cm less than desired length from underarm.

Change to smaller DPNs needles and work 2 rounds as established. Using the Tubular Bind-Off method, BO all sts in pattern.

Finishing

Weave in end, soak, and gently block to measurement.

詳細情報

Yarn

Worsted weight yarn

約1320 (1390, 1580, 1700, 1920, 2040) yards / 1210 (1275, 1450, 1560, 1760, 1870) m

Brooklyn Tweed Shelter (100 % American Targhee - Columbia Wool; 140 yards / 50g), 10 (10, 12, 13, 14, 15)カセ

サンプル色はCamper

Needles

1 x US 7 (4.5 mm) 32″ / 80 cm (またはそれ以上の長さ)の輪針

1 x US 7 (4.5 mm) 16″ / 40 cmの輪針

1 x US 4 (3.5 mm) 16″ / 40 cmの輪針

1 x US 7 (4.5 mm) 4本棒針

1 x US 4 (3.5 mm) 4本棒針

または, ゲージが取れる太さの針

Gauge (ブロッキング後)

US 7 (4.5 mm)の針を使用し, 1x1のねじりゴム編みで 26目 & 31段 = 10 cm

Sizes

出来上がり寸法: 胸囲 XS (S, M, L, XL, XXL) = 86 (91, 98, 107, 117, 123) cm

モデルはSサイズを着用し, 余裕として+9 cm

Tools

目数マーカー , 綴じ針, 縄編み針, 別糸

Stitch Guide

Special Stitch (SS): (3目使う) 左針に目を置いたまま, 3番目の目を2番目の目に被せる, 2番目の目を1番目の目に被せる. その後でこの目を(K1, YO, K1).

ねじり1目ゴム編み (輪編み):

周1: *(K1tbl, P1) または *(P1, K1tbl), *以降を最後まで繰り返す.

周1を繰り返す.

ねじり1目ゴム編み (往復編み):

段1: *(K1tbl, P1) または *(P1, K1tbl), *以降を最後まで繰り返す.

段2: *(K1, P1tbl) または * (P1tbl, K1), *以降を最後まで繰り返す.

段1と2を繰り返す.

1/1/1 LPT: CNに1目滑らせ手前に置く, 次の目を2つ目のCNに滑らせ後ろ側に置く, K1 tbl, 後ろ側のCNの目をP1, 手前側のCNの目をK1 tbl.

1/1/1 RPT: 2目をCNに滑らせ後ろ側に置く, K1 tbl, CNから1目を左針に滑らせCNを手前側に移動する, P1, CNの目をK1 tbl.

Skill Level

Note

このセーターはトップダウンで, 輪で編み進める, 綴じはぎはない. 作り目は襟ぐりの端になる. ヨークを編んだ後, 身頃と袖を分けて, 袖の目を別糸またはホルダーに休めておく. 休めておいた袖の目も, 同様にマジックループまたは4本棒針を使って輪で編む. 後ろ襟ぐりと後ろの裾は, ねじり1目ゴム編みを続けながら引返し編みを使って編む. ゴム編みの作り目とゴム編み止めも, セーターの端が丸く続く様子を表すデザインの一端を担っている. 目数マーカーは後ろ襟ぐりの中心に付ける.

編みかた

Yoke

襟

細い方の針を使い指で掛ける作り目で, CO 128 (136, 136, 136, 144, 144)目. PM, 輪にする.

ねじり1目ゴム編み(K1tbl, P)で2周編む.

XS (S, M, L, XL)サイズのみ

太い方の針に替えて, ねじり1目ゴム編みで18周編む. 計128 (136, 136, 136,144)目.

XXLサイズのみ

太い方の針に替えてねじり1目ゴム編みで5周編む.

増目周: (K1tbl, P1)を14回編む, 1目に(K1tbl, P1, K1tbl)を編み入れ, (P1, K1tbl)を7回編み, 1目に(P1, K1tbl, P1)を編み入れ, (K1tbl, P1)を28回編む, 1目に(K1tbl, P1, K1tbl)を編み入れ, (P1, K1tbl)を7回編み, 1目に(P1, K1tbl, P1)を編み入れ, (K1tbl, P1)を14回編む. 計152目.

ねじり1目ゴム編みで5周編む.

増目周: (K1tbl, P1)を14回編む, K1tbl, 1目に(P1, K1tbl, P1)を編み入れ, (K1tbl, P1)を8回編み, 1目に(K1tbl, P1, K1tbl)を編み入れ, (P1, K1tbl)を29回編み, 1目に(P1, K1tbl, P1)を編み入れ, (K1tbl, P1)を8回編み, 1目に(K1tbl, P1, K1tbl)を編み入れ, (P1, K1tbl)を14回編む, P1. 計160目.

ねじり1目ゴム編みで6周編む.

計128 (136, 136, 136, 144, 160)目.

後ろ襟ぐりの引返し

Note: 以下のように引返しを行うが, ここでは"ラップ"の代わりにYOを使い, 次にその掛け目を編む際, 次の目とパターン通りにK2tog tblまたはSSKをする.

引返し段 1: (K1tbl, P1)を4回編む, TW.

引返し段2: YO, (K1, P1tbl)を8回編む, TW.

引返し段3から段10: YO, 最後の折り返しの8目後までパターン通りに編む, TW.

引返し段 11 to 14: YO, 最後の折り返しの8 (10, 10, 10, 12, 12)目後までパターン通りに編む, TW.

引返し段15: YO, Mまでパターン通りに編む. 最後のYOは次の周でYOの1目前の目とP2togする.

ヨーク

セットアップ周: *(K1tbl, P1)を4回編む, PM, *以降を最後まで繰り返す.

計128 (136, 136, 136, 144, 160)目.

XS, Sサイズのみ (チャート1)

チャート1の周1から周46を編む. 計288 (306)目.

Sサイズのみ

周46をあと4回編む. 合計50周.

M, L, XL, XXLサイズのみ (チャート2)

チャート2の周1から周56を編む.

計340 (340, 360, 400)目.

周56をあと0 (2, 6, 10)回編む. 合計56 (58, 62, 66) 周.

周47 (51, 57, 59, 63, 67): 全てP.

XS, Mサイズのみ

周48 (58): 全てK.

S, L, XL, XXLサイズのみ

増目周52 (60, 64, 68): Pfbを使って均等に2 (8, 16, 8)目増目しながら, 全てP.

計288 (308, 340, 348, 376, 408)目.

周49 (53, 59, 61, 65, 69): *(K2tog tbl, YO), *以降を最後まで繰り返す.

周50 (54, 60, 62, 66, 70): *(P1, P1tbl), *以降を最後まで繰り返す.

袖と身頃を分ける

セットアップ周51 (55, 61, 63, 67, 71): P45 (48, 53, 56, 62, 66)目, 54 (58, 64, 62, 64, 72)目を別糸に休ませる, 巻き増し目でCO 20 (20, 20, 24, 24, 24)目, P90 (96, 106, 112, 124, 132)目, 54 (58, 64, 62, 64, 72)目を別糸に休ませる, 巻き増し目でCO 20 (20, 20, 24, 24, 24)目, P45 (48, 53, 56, 62, 66)目. 計220 (232, 252, 272, 296, 312)目.

ねじり1目ゴム編みで5周編む.

XS, Sサイズのみ

周57 (61): P1, *(SS, P1) *以降を最後まで繰り返す.

M, L, XL, XXLのみ

周67 (69,73,77): *(SS, P1) *以降を最後まで繰り返す.

全てのサイズ

ねじり1目ゴム編みで5周編む.

XS, Sサイズのみ

周63 (67): P1, *(SS, P1) *以降を最後まで繰り返す.

M, L, XL, XXLサイズのみ

周73 (75,79,83): *(SS, P1) *以降を最後まで繰り返す

全てのサイズ

ねじり1目ゴム編みで5周編む.

周69 (73, 79, 81, 85, 89)と70 (74, 80, 82, 86, 90): 全てP.

周71 (75, 81, 83, 87, 91): *(K2tog tbl, YO), *以降を最後まで繰り返す.

周72 (76, 82, 84, 88, 92)と73 (77, 83, 85, 89, 93): 全てP.

XS, Sサイズのみ

Pで編み始めて, ねじり1目ゴム編みで7周編む.

M, L, XL, XXLサイズのみ

K1tblで編み始めて, ねじり1目ゴム編みで7 (7, 9, 11)周編む.

身頃の増目

XS, Sサイズのみ

周81 (85): (P1, K1tbl)を10 (11)回編む, 1目に(P1, K1tbl, P1)を編み入れ, (K1tbl, P1)を34 (35)回編む, 1目に(K1tbl, P1, K1tbl)を編み入れ, (P1, K1tbl)を20 (22)回編む, 1目に(P1,

K1tbl, P1)を編み入れ, (K1tbl, P1)を34 (35)回編む, 1目に(K1tbl, P1, K1tbl)を編み入れ, (P1, K1tbl)を10 (11)回編む. 計228 (240)目.

M, L, XL, XXLサイズのみ

周91 (93, 99, 105): (K1tbl, P1)を11 (12, 12, 13)回編む, 1目に(K1tbl, P1, K1tbl)を編み入れ, (P1, K1tbl)を40 (43, 49, 51)回編む, 1目に(P1, K1tbl, P1)を編み入れ, (K1tbl, P1)を22 (24, 24, 26)回編む, 1目に(K1tbl, P1, K1tbl)を編み入れ, (P1, K1tbl)を40 (43, 49, 51)回編む, 1目に(P1, K1tbl, P1)を編み入れ, (K1tbl, P1)を11 (12, 12, 13)回編む. 計260 (280, 304, 320)目.

全てのサイズ

ねじり1目ゴム編みでパターン通りに9周編む.

XS, Sサイズのみ

周91 (95): (P1, K1tbl)を10 (11)回編む, P1, 1目に(K1tbl, P1, K1tbl)を編み入れ, (P1, K1tbl)を35 (36)回編む, 1目に(P1, K1tbl, P1)を編み入れ, (K1tbl, P1)を21 (23)回編む, 1目に(K1tbl, P1, K1tbl)を編み入れ, (P1, K1tbl)を35 (36)回編む, 1目に(P1, K1tbl, P1)を編み入れ, (K1tbl, P1)を10 (11)回編む, K1tbl. 計236 (248)目.

M, L, XL, XXLサイズのみ

周101 (103, 109, 115): (K1tbl, P1)を11 (12, 12, 13)回編む, 1目に(P1, K1tbl, P1)を編み入れ, (K1tbl, P1)を41 (44, 50, 52)回編む, 1目に(K1tbl, P1, K1tbl)を編み入れ, (P1, K1tbl)を23 (25, 25, 27)回編む, 1目に(P1, K1tbl, P1)を編み入れ, (K1tbl, P1)を41 (44, 50, 52)回編む, 1目に(K1tbl, P1, K1tbl)を編み入れ, (P1, K1tbl)を11 (12, 12, 13)回編む, P1. 計268 (288, 312, 328)目.

全てのサイズ

ねじり1目ゴム編みでパターン通りに13周編む.

XS, Sサイズのみ

周105 (109): (P1, K1tbl)を11 (12)回編む, 1目に(P1, K1tbl, P1)編み入れ, (K1tbl, P1)を36 (37)回編む, 1目に(K1tbl, P1, K1tbl)編み入れ, (P1, K1tbl)を22 (24)回編む, 1目に(P1, K1tbl, P1)編み入れ, (K1tbl, P1)を36 (37)回編む, 1目に(K1tbl, P1, K1tbl)編み入れ, (P1, K1tbl)を11 (12)回編む. 計244 (256)目.

M, L, XL, XXLサイズのみ

周115 (117, 123, 129): (K1tbl, P1)を12 (13, 13, 14)回編む, 1目に(K1tbl, P1, K1tbl)を編み入れ, (P1, K1tbl)を42 (45, 51, 53)回編む, 1目に(P1, K1tbl, P1)を編み入れ, (K1tbl, P1)を24 (26, 26, 28)回編む, 1目に(K1tbl, P1, K1tbl)を編み入れ, (P1, K1tbl)を42 (45, 51, 53)回編む, 1目に(P1, K1tbl, P1)を編み入れ, (K1tbl, P1)を12 (13, 13, 14)回編む. 計276 (296, 320, 336)目.

全てのサイズ

脇の作り目からの長さが38 (38, 41, 41, 43, 43) cmになるまで, ねじり1目ゴム編みでパターン通りに編む.

後ろ身頃の裾の引返し

XS, Sサイズのみ

引返し段1: (P1, K1tbl)を41 (44)回編む, W&T.

引返し段2: (P1tbl, K1)を82(88)回編む, W&T.

引返し段3, 4: ねじり1目ゴム編みでパターン通りに最後にラップした目の3目前まで編む, W&T.

引返し段5, 6: ねじり1目ゴム編みでパターン通りに最後にラップした目の2目前まで編む, W&T.

引返し段7: 整理編みをしながら, ねじり1目ゴム編みでパターン通りにMまで編む.

M, L, XL, XXLサイズのみ

引返し段1: (K1tbl, P1)を47 (51, 56, 59)回編む, W&T.

引返し段2: (K1, P1tbl)を94 (102, 112, 118)回編む, W&T.

引返し段3, 4: ねじり1目ゴム編みでパターン通りに最後にラップした目の3目前まで編む, W&T.

引返し段5, 6: ねじり1目ゴム編みでパターン通りに最後にラップした目の2目前まで編む, W&T.

引返し段7: 整理編みをしながら, ねじり1目ゴム編みでMまで編む.

全てのサイズ

ねじり1目ゴム編みでパターン通りに2周編む. 1目ゴム編み止めで全ての目をBO.

袖

片袖の54 (58, 64, 62, 64, 72)目を, US 7 (4.5mm)の4本棒針か細い方の針に戻す. 糸を付けて脇下中心から編み始める, 10 (10, 10, 12, 12, 12)目拾う, 袖の目をパターン通りに編む, 脇下から10 (10, 10, 12, 12, 12)目拾う. PM, 輪にする. 計74 (78, 84, 86, 88, 96)目.

ねじり1目ゴム編み(K1tbl, P1) で8 (7, 6, 6, 5)周編む.

減目周: K1tbl, K2tog, ねじり1目ゴム編みでMの2目前まで編む, SSK. 2目減目. 計72 (76, 82, 84, 86, 94)目.

最後の9 (8, 7, 7, 6)周をあと10 (12, 13, 14, 15, 17)回編む. 計52 (52, 56, 56, 56, 60)目.

ねじり1目ゴム編みで26 (24, 34, 28, 22, 26)周編む.

細い方の4本棒針に替えてパターン通りに2周編む.1目ゴム編み止めで全ての目をBO.

仕上げ

糸始末をし, 寸法通りにブロッキングする.

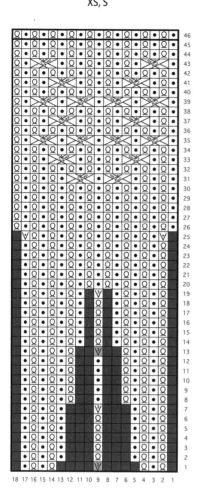

XS, S   M, L, XL, XXL

	K tbl
⟨⟩	1/1/1 RPT
⟨⟩	1/1/1 LPT
•	P
☐	Repetition / 繰返し
Ⅴ	P tbl into front and K tbl in the back 前のループに P tbl し後ろループに K tbl
Ⅴ	K tbl into front and P tbl in the back 前のループに K tbl し後ろループに P tbl
■	no stitch 目がない
Ⅴ	(K1tbl, P1, K1tbl) in 1 st / 1 目に (K1tbl, P1, K1tbl) を編み入れる
Ⅴ	(P1, K1tbl, P1) in 1 st / / 1 目に (P1, K1tbl, P1) を編み入れる

Kew by Nele Redweik

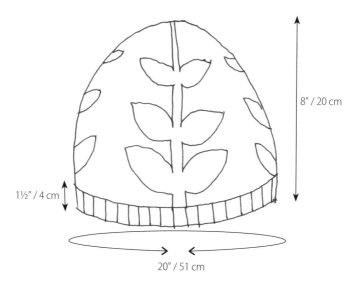

8" / 20 cm

1½" / 4 cm

20" / 51 cm

Specifications

Yarn
DK weight yarn

Approximately 145 yards, 133 m

1 skein of Brooklyn Tweed Arbor (100% American Targhee wool; 145 yards / 133 m, 50g)

Sample shown in color Degas

Lace weight yarn

Approximately 145 yards, 133 m

1 ball of Isager Silk Mohair (75% kid mohair, 25% silk; 232 yards / 212 m, 25g)

Sample shown in color 62

Please note: Both yarns are held together throughout the hat.

Needles
A US 8 (5 mm) 16" circular needle

A US 6 (4 mm) 16" circular needle or two sizes smaller than gauge needle

A set of US 8 (5 mm) double pointed needles (DPNs)

Or, needle required to obtain gauge

Gauge (after blocking)
19 stitches & 31 rows = 4" / 10 cm in St st with US 8 (5 mm) needle

Size
Finished measurements: circumference: 20" / 51cm, height: 8" / 20 cm

Tools
Stitch markers (3), tapestry needle

Stitch Guide
PbKf: Purl into back of stitch, move yarn to back and knit into front of the same stitch

Skill Level
●●●○○

Notes
This hat is knit in the round from the brim up, switching from the 16" circular needles to DPNs as needed.

Instruction

With smaller needle and holding one strand each of Arbor and Lace Mohair together, CO 100 sts using the Long Tail method. PM and join in the round, careful not to twist the stitches.

Next Rnd: K2, *P1, K3, repeat from * to 2 sts before M, P1, K1.

Knit in established 3 x 1 rib for 1½" / 4 cm (approximately 13 rounds).

First Leaf Pattern
Switch to larger needle.

Rnd 1: P12, K9, P12, PM, Pfb, P10, K9, P12, PM, Pfb, P10, K9, P2tog, P3, P2tog, P6, P2tog, SM. 99 sts.

Rnd 2: Work row 2 of First Leaf Pattern Chart 3 times, SM.

Rnds 3 - 18: Work next row of First Leaf Pattern Chart 3 times, SM. Total 99 sts.

First leaf pattern

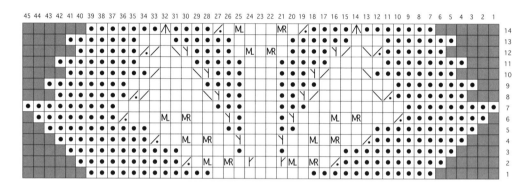

Second leaf pattern

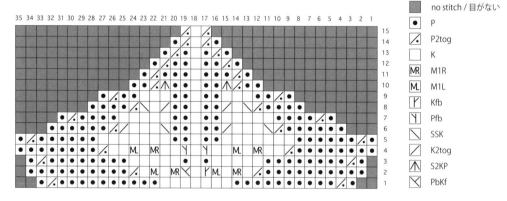

Third leaf pattern

▦	no stitch / 目がない
•	P
╱.	P2tog
□	K
M̄R	M1R
M̄L	M1L
⋎	Kfb
Ⴘ	Pfb
╲	SSK
╱	K2tog
⋀	S2KP
⋈	PbKf

Second Leaf Pattern

Rnd 1: Work row 1 of Second Leaf Pattern Chart 3 times, SM.

Rnds 2 - 14: Work next row of Second Leaf Pattern Chart 3 times, SM. Total 99 sts.

Third Leaf Pattern and Decrease Section

Rnd 1: Work row 1 of Third Leaf Pattern Chart 3 times, SM.

Rnds 2 - 14: Work next row of Third Leaf Pattern Chart 3 times, SM.

Rnd 15: Work row 15 of Third Leaf Pattern Chart 3 times, RM. Total 9 sts.

Finishing

Break yarn, leaving a 6" / 15 cm tail. Use tapestry needle to thread tail through remaining 9 sts twice, pulling tight to avoid a hole. Weave in ends. Block.

詳細情報

Yarn

DK weight yarn

約145 yards, 133 m

Brooklyn Tweed Arbor (100% American Targhee wool; 145 yards / 133 m, 50g), 1カセ

サンプル色はDegas

Lace weight yarn

約145 yards, 133 m

Isager Silk Mohair (75% kid mohair, 25% silk; 232 yards / 212 m, 25g), 1玉

サンプル色は62

Note: 常に2本取りで編む.

Needles

1 x US 8 (5 mm) 16"の輪針

1 x US 6 (4 mm) 16"の輪針またはゲージに合わせた輪針より2サイズ細い輪針

1 x US 6 (4 mm) 4本棒針(DPNs)

またはゲージに合わせた太さの針

Gauge (ブロッキング後)

US 8 (5 mm)の針を使用し, メリヤス編みで19目 & 31段 = 10 cm

Size

できあがり寸法: 頭囲 51cm, 高さ 20 cm

Tools

目数マーカー (3), 綴じ針

Stitch Guide

PbKf: 後ろ側のループに針を入れてP, 糸を後ろに持って行き, 同じ目にK.

Skill Level

Note

この帽子はブリム(つば)から頭頂に向かって輪で編んでいく. 必要に応じて, 輪針から4本棒針に替えて編む.

編みかた

細い方の針を用い, ArberとLace Mohairの2本取りで, 指で掛ける作り目でCO 100目. PM, ねじれないように気を付けて輪にする.

次の周: K2, *P1, K3, *以降をMから2目前まで繰り返す, P1, K1.

3 x 1のゴム編みをパターン通りに4 cm編む (約13周).

First leaf pattern

太い方の針に替える.

周1: P12, K9, P12, PM, Pfb, P10, K9, P12, PM, Pfb, P10, K9, P2tog, P3, P2tog, P6, P2tog, SM. 計99目.

周2: First leaf patternのチャートの段2を3回編む, SM.

周3 - 18: First leaf patternのチャートの次の段を3回編む, SM.

計99目.

Second leaf pattern

周1: Second leaf patternの段1を3回編む, SM.

周2 - 14: Second leaf patternの次の段を3回編む, SM.

計99目.

Third leaf patternと減目セクション

周1: Third leaf patternのチャートの段1を3回編む, SM.

周2 - 14: Third leaf patternのチャートの次の段を3回編む, SM.

周15: Third leaf patternのチャートの段15を3回編む, RM.

計9目.

仕上げ

糸を15 cmくらい残して切る. 綴じ針を使って残っている9目に2度通して穴を塞ぐようにきつく引っ張る. 糸始末をする. 形を整えるようにブロッキングする.

Bavaria by Isabell Kraemer

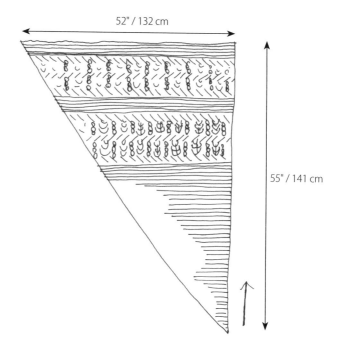

52" / 132 cm

55" / 141 cm

Specifications

Yarn
Worsted weight yarn

Approximately 1080 yards, 990 m

9 skeins of Quince & Co. Owl (50% Wool, 50% Alpaca; 120 yards / 110m, 50g)

Sample is shown in Tawny

Needles
A US 8 (5 mm) 32" / 80 cm (or longer) circular needle

Or, needle required to obtain gauge

Gauge (after blocking)
15 stitches & 29 rows = 4" / 10 cm in Garter Stitch with US 8 (5 mm) needle

Size
Approximately 52" / 132 cm wide at right edge, 55" / 141 cm along top edge

Tools
Stitch marker (1), cable needle, tapestry needle, blocking tools

Stitch Guide
MB: (K, P, K) in 1 stitch, turn. P1, (P, YO, P) in 1 stitch, P1, turn. K5, turn. P2tog, P1, P2tog, turn. S2KP.

1/2 RC: Slip 2 stitches to CN and hold in back; K1; K2 from CN.

1/2 LC: Slip 1 stitch to cable needle and hold in front; K2; K1 from cable needle.

Skill Level
●●○○○

Notes
Knitting starts at the tip of the left edge and ends on the full side of the right edge. Increases are worked at the end of every other row to achieve an asymmetrical triangular shape. A two stitch I-Cord is worked at the edge for a clean finish. The body of the shawl consists of a combination of Garter Stitch and two wide pattern bands.

Instruction

With Long Tail Cast On method, CO 6 sts using US 8 (5 mm) needle.

Knit 1 WS row.

Garter Stitch Body
Row 1 (RS): Sl 1 wyf, K to last 2 sts, Kfb, K1. Total 7 sts.

Row 2 (WS): K to last 2 sts, Sl 1 wyf, K1.

Repeat rows 1 and 2 until you have 112 sts (105 repeats)

Pattern Band 1

Set up row (RS): Sl 1 wyf, K3, PM, K to last 2 sts, Kfb, K1. Total 113 sts.

Next row (WS): K to M, SM, K2, Sl 1 wyf, K1.

Work rows 1 to 70 from Chart A. Total 148 sts.

Work rows 1 and 2 of Garter Stitch Body 7 times. Total 155 sts.

Pattern Band 2

Work rows 1 to 70 from Chart B. Total 190 sts.

Work rows 1 and 2 of Garter Stitch Body 5 times.

BO all stitches .

Carefully weave in all ends and block shawl.

詳細情報

Yarn

Worsted weight yarn

約1080 yards, 990 m

Quince & Co. Owl (50% Wool, 50% Alpaca; 120 yards / 110m / 50g), 9カセ

サンプル色はTawny

Needles

1 x US 8 (5 mm) 80 cmもしくはそれ以上の長さの輪針

または, ゲージが取れる太さの針

Gauge (ブロッキング後)

US 8 (5 mm)の針を使用し, ガーター編みで15目 & 29段 = 10 cm

Size

約 幅132 cm, 高さ141 cm

Tools

目数マーカー (1), 縄編み針, とじ針, ブロッキング用品

Stitch Guide

MB: 次の目に(K, P, K)を編み入れる, 編地を返す. P1, 次の目に(P, YO, P)を編み入れる, P1, 編地を返す. K5, 編地を返す. P2tog, P1, P2tog, 編地を返す. 中上3目一度.

1/2 RC: 縄編み針に2目移し後ろへ置く, K1, 縄編み針からK2.

1/2 LC: 縄編み針に1目移し手前へ置く, K2, 縄編み針からK1.

Skill Level

Note

先端から編み始め, 各段の最後で増目ですることによりアシンメトリーな三角形を作る. 端目は2目のI-Cordを用い, ショール本体はガーターと2つのチャートの組み合わせで構成されている.

編みかた

US 8 (5 mm)の針を用い, 指に掛ける作り目でCO 6.

WS段をKで1段編む.

ガーター部分

段 1 (RS): Sl 1 wyf, 最後の2目までK, Kfb, K1. 計7目

段 2 (WS): 最後の2目までK, Sl 1 wyf, K1.

段1 と2を112目になるまで繰り返す. 計112 目 (105回繰り返し)

模様編み1

セットアップ段 (RS): Sl 1 wyf, K3, PM, 最後の2目までK, Kfb, K1. 計113 目

次の段 (WS): MまでK, SM, K2, Sl 1 wyf, K1.

Chart Aの段1 から70を編む. 計148 目

ガーター部分の段1と2を7回繰り返す. 計155 目

模様編み2

Chart Bの段1 から70を編む. 計190 目

ガーター部分の段1と2を5回繰り返す.

全ての目をKで編みながらBO.

糸始末をしブロッキングする.

Chart A

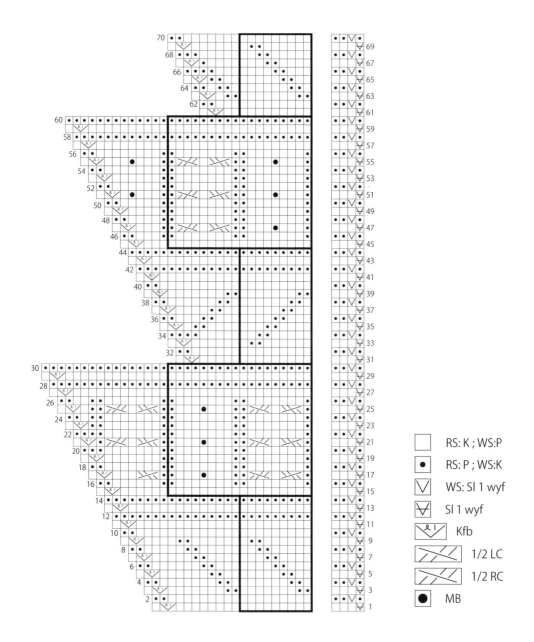

RS: K ; WS:P

● RS: P ; WS:K

WS: Sl 1 wyf

Sl 1 wyf

Kfb

1/2 LC

1/2 RC

● MB

Chart B

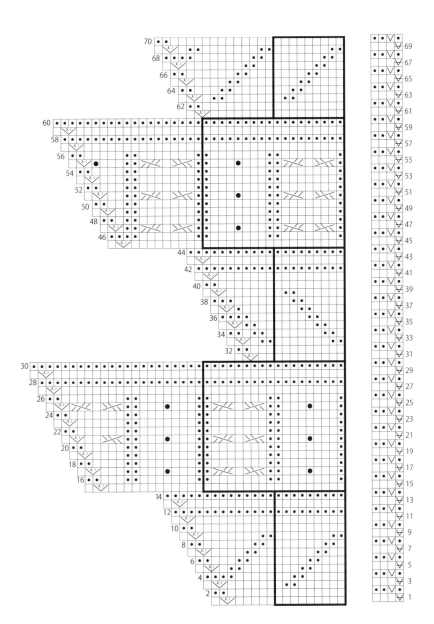

Pink Pine Pair by Nataliya Sinelshchikova

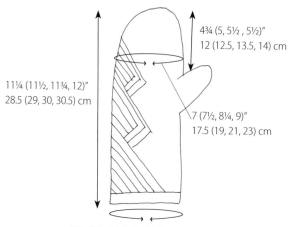

4¾ (5, 5½ , 5½)"
12 (12.5, 13.5, 14) cm

11¼ (11½, 11¾, 12)"
28.5 (29, 30, 30.5) cm

7 (7½, 8¼, 9)"
17.5 (19, 21, 23) cm

7¾ (8½, 9¼, 10)"/ 20 (21.5, 23.5, 25.5) cm

Specifications

Yarn
Sport weight yarn

(MC) Approximately 120 (135, 165, 195) yards, 110 (125, 150, 180) m

(CC) Approximately 110 yards, 100 m

2 skeins of Quince & Co. Chickadee (100% american wool; 181 yards / 166 m, 50g)

Sample is shown in Iceland 1 skein (MC), Rosa Rugosa 1 skein (CC).

Needles
A US 3 (3.25 mm) 40" / 100 cm (or longer) circular needle for magic loop method or a set of double pointed needles (DPNs)

A US 1 (2.25 mm) 40" / 100 cm (or longer) circular needle for magic loop method or a set of double pointed needles (DPNs)

Or, needles required to obtain gauge

Gauge (after blocking)
27.5 stitches & 39 rows = 4" / 10 cm in St st with US 3 (3.25 mm) needle knitted in the round.

Sizes
Finished palm circumference on widest part: XS (S, M, L) = 7 (7½, 8 ¼, 9)" / 17.5 (19, 21, 23) cm

Sample shown in size S

Tools
Stitch marker (1), tapestry needle, waste yarn

Stitch Guide
RT2: K2tog leaving sts on LH needle, then K the first st again, slipping sts off needle.

LT2: Skip next st, K following st tbl leaving st on LH needle, then K skipped st through front loop, slipping sts off needle.

LT2togYO: Left twist 2, knitting the twist st together with YO. Skip next st, K following st through back of loop together with YO leaving sts on LH needle, then K skipped st through front loop, slipping sts off needle.

RT2chMC: Right twist 2 with color change from CC to MC. With CC K2tog leaving sts on LH needle, then change from CC to MC, K the first st again with MC, slipping sts off needle.

LT2chCC: Left twist 2 with color change from MC to CC. Skip next st, with MC K following st through back of loop leaving st on LH needle, then change from MC to CC, then with CC K skipped st through front loop, slipping sts off needle.

Kitchener Stitch without ears: Before starting to work Kitchener Stitch, divide stitches equally between front and back needles. Yarn tail comes from behind. Insert tapestry needle into the first stitch on front needle as if to knit, slide the stitch off the needle and insert tapestry needle into second stitch as if to purl (without sliding it from the front needle) and pull the yarn through both stitches. Keeping the yarn under the needle tips, insert tapestry needle into the first stitch on the back needle as if to purl, slide the stitch from the back needle, insert tapestry needle into second stitch as if to knit (without sliding it from the back needle) and pull the yarn through. Bring the yarn to the front underneath the tips of needles. Continue working the Kitchener Stitch as usual, until one stitch left on each needle. Slip these stitches off the needles, and weave in the end.

Skill Level
●●●●○

Notes

Mittens are knit from the bottom up using the Intarsia technique. In order to knit Intarsia in the round, odd rounds are worked on RS and even rounds are worked on WS using the Invisible Join method. Therefore the chart is read from right to left for odd rows and from left to right for even rows. The mittens can be knit using the Magic Loop method or by using DPNs.

When switching colors, make sure to twist yarns in order to avoid forming holes.

Instruction

Hem

With Crochet Provisional Cast-On and waste yarn CO 54 (58, 64, 68) sts using smaller needle. PM and join in the round.

With CC K 6 rounds, P 1 round, K 6 rounds (13 rounds in total), RM.

Fold up the fabric. WSs should be facing each other. Unravel cast-on edge and pick up sts using spare needle. Hold front needle (with working sts) parallel to back needle (with picked up sts). Using larger size needle K 1 st from the front needle together with 1 st from the back needle. Repeat to the end of round.

Wrist

Turn the piece to work from the WS.

Note: A marker indicates end of rounds. RM after finishing each round.

Set-up Rnd (WS): In CC YO, PM, P24, join MC, P6 (10, 16, 20) in MC, join new thread of CC, P23 in CC, P2tog, RM, TW.

Rnd 1 (RS): In CC YO, PM, RT2 11times, RT2chMC, K6 (10, 16, 20), LT2chCC, LT2 10 times, LT2togYO, RM, TW.

Rnd 2 (WS): In CC YO, PM, P23, change to MC, P8 (12, 18, 22), change to CC, P22, P2tog, RM, TW.

Rnd 3 (RS): In CC YO, PM, K1, RT2 10 times, RT2chMC, K8 (12, 18, 22), LT2chCC, LT2 10 times, SSK, RM, TW.

Rnd 4 (WS): In CC YO, PM, P22, change to MC, P10 (14, 20, 24), change to CC, P21, P2tog, RM, TW.

Continue Chart 01 from Rnd 5 for both hands.

Pay extra attention to highlighted areas while working Rnds 21–28.

Palm

Continue by following Chart 02LEFT for left hand and 02RIGHT for right hand.

Pay extra attention to highlighted areas while working Rnds 9–16.

After finishing the chart, 61 (65, 71, 75) sts on needles.

Fingers

Division for thumb and fingers:

Rnd 1 (RS): In CC YO, PM, RT2 5 times, RT2chMC, K11 (13, 15, 17), transfer next 15 (15, 17, 17) sts to waste yarn, using Crochet Provisional Cast-On and waste yarn make 4 sts and transfer them to LH needle, then K these stitches, K11 (13, 15, 17), LT2chCC, LT2 4 times, LT2togYO, RM, TW. 50 (54, 58, 62) sts on needles.

Rnd 2 (WS): In CC YO, PM, P11, change to MC, P26 (30, 34, 38), change to CC, P10, P2tog, RM, TW.

Continue by following Chart 03 for both hands until Rnd 19.

Rnd 19 (RS): In CC YO, PM, K2tog, change to MC, K46 (50, 54, 58), change to CC, SSSK, do not TW, break CC yarn threads. 48 (52, 56, 60) sts on needles.

Continue knitting in the round with MC.

The mittens are designed for a standard finger length, if you have longer fingers add the necessary number of rounds between Rnds 20 and 26.

Rnds 27–28 to be knit only for sizes S, M, and L.

Rnds 29–30 to be knit only for sizes M and L.

Rnds 31–32 to be knit only for size L.

Knit the last round (50th for sizes XS and S, 51th for sizes M and L) using smaller size needles.

12 (16, 16, 20) sts on needles after finishing chart.

Graft remaining sts using Kitchener Stitch without ears.

Thumb

Note: Twist and pick up stitches from gaps between stitches on waste yarn and CO to avoid loose stitches.

Do not attach yarn yet.

Transfer 15 (15, 17, 17) sts from waste yarn, pick up 3 sts from the gap, unravel cast on edge and pick up 4 sts, pick up 2 sts from the gap, PM. 24 (24, 26, 26) sts on needles.

Attach MC.

Rnds 1–4: K all sts.

Rnd 5: K15 (15, 17, 17), SSK, K until 2 sts before M, K2tog. Repeat Rnds 1–5 2 more times. 18 (18, 20, 20) sts on needles.

K 13 (15, 17, 17) rounds. Then K2tog 9 (9, 10, 10) times.

Break yarn. Pass the end through remaining sts and pull tightly to close a gap.

Finishing

Close the gaps (if there are any) at the joint of thumb using yarn tail. Weave in ends with tapestry needle. Wet block to measurements with blockers or blocking pins.

詳細情報

Yarn

Sport weight yarn

(MC) 約 120 (135, 165, 195) yards, 110 (125, 150, 180) m

(CC) 約 110 yards, 100 m

Quince & Co. Chickadee (100% american wool; 181 yards / 166 m, 50g)

サンプル色はIceland 1カセ (MC), Rosa Rugosa 1カセ (CC).

Needles

1 x US 3 (3.25 mm) 40" / 100 cm以上の輪針, もしくは4本棒針

1 x US 1 (2.25 mm) 40" / 100 cm以上の輪針, もしくは4本棒針

または, ゲージが取れる太さの針

Gauge (ブロッキング後)

US 3 (3.25 mm) の針を使用し, メリヤス編みの輪編みで27.5目 & 39段 = 10 cm

Sizes

出来上がり寸法:手のひらの一番広い部分の周囲 XS (S, M, L) = 17.5 (19, 21, 23) cm

サンプルはSサイズ

Tools

マーカー (1), 綴じ針, 別糸

Stitch Guide

RT2: 左上1目交差

LT2: 右上1目交差

LT2togYO: 次の目を飛ばし, その次の目をねじり目を編むように針を入れ隣のかけ目と共に2目一度する. そのまま目を左針から落とさずに飛ばした最初の目を表編みし, 3目(2目とかけ目)を左針から外す.

RT2chMC: CCでK2tog, 目を左針から落とさずにMCに変えて右側の目をもう一度K, 目を左針から外す.

LT2chCC: 次の目を飛ばし, MCでその次の目をねじり表目, 目を左針から落とさずにCCに変えて飛ばした目をK, 左針から目を外す.

Kitchener stitch without ears: 残っている目を均等に2つの針に分け, 前後に持つ. 糸は奥におく. とじ針を手前の針の最初の目に表目を編むように入れ, 目を針から落とす. とじ針を次の目に裏目を編むように入れ(目は針に残したまま), 糸を引き締める. 糸端を針の下にをくぐらせてとじ針を奥の針の最初の目に裏目を編むように入れ, 目を針から落とす. 次の目に表目を編むように入れ(目は針に残したまま), 糸を引き締める.あとは普通のメリヤスはぎの要領で両方の針に1目ずつ残るまで行う. 残った2目を針から落とし, 糸端を処理する

Skill Level

●●●●○

Note

手首からインターシアの技法を使いながらボトムアップで編む. 手のひらはInvisible Joinという方法を使いながら往復編み, 途中から輪編みで指先を編む. 往復編みの際はチャートは奇数段では右から左へ, 偶数段では左から右へ読む. ミトンはマジックループで輪針で編んでも, 4本棒針で編んでもよい. 色を替える時は穴が空くのを防ぐために糸同士を絡める。

編みかた

US 8 (5 mm)の針を用い, 指に掛ける作り目でCO 6.
WS段をKで1段編む.

ヘム部分

段1 (RS): SI 1 wyf, 最後の2目までK, Kfb, K1. 計7目

段2 (WS): 最後の2目までK, SI 1 wyf, K1.

小さい方の針を用い, Crochet Provisional Cast-Onと別糸でCO 54 (58, 64, 68)目. PM, 輪にする.

CCでK 6周, P 1周, K 6 周 (計13周), RM.

表が外側になるように折り返し, 作り目を解きながら空いている針に目を取る. 糸が繋がっている針が手前, 作り目から取った目が掛かった針を奥に持ち, 大きい方の針で手前の針から1目, 奥の針から1目取り2目一度する. これを周の最後まで繰り返す.

手首

編み地を裏側に返す.

Note: YOの後に周の最後がわかりやすいようマーカーを入れるが, 2目一度をした後はマーカーを外すとよい.

セットアップ周 (WS): CCで YO, PM, P24, MCに替えてP6 (10, 16, 20), 新しいCCをつなぎP23, P2tog, RM, TW.

周1 (RS): CCで YO, PM, RT2 を11回, RT2chMC, K6 (10, 16, 20), LT2chCC, LT2を10回, LT2togYO, RM, TW.

周2 (WS): CCでYO, PM, P23, MCに替えてP8 (12, 18, 22), CCに替えてP22, P2tog, RM, TW.

周3 (RS): In CC YO, PM, K1, RT2を10回, RT2chMC, K8 (12, 18, 22), LT2chCC, LT2を10回, SSK, RM, TW.

周4 (WS): In CC YO, PM, P22, MCに替えて, P10 (14, 20, 24), CCに替えて, P21, P2tog, RM, TW.

周21−28の太線で囲っている部分に注意しながら, 続けてChart 01の周5から両手共に編む.

手のひら

続けて, 周9−16の太線で囲っている部分に注意しながら左手はChart 02LEFT, 右手は02RIGHTを編む. 計61 (65, 71, 75)目.

指先

親指を分ける

周 1 (RS): CCでYO, PM, RT2を5回, RT2chMC, K11 (13, 15, 17), 次の15 (15, 17, 17)目を別糸に休める, Crochet Provisional Cast-Onで別糸を使って左針にCO 4目し, この4目をK, K11 (13, 15, 17), LT2chCC, LT2を4回, LT2togYO, RM, TW. 計50 (54, 58, 62)目.

周 2(WS): CCでYO, PM, P11, MCに替えて, P26(30, 34, 38), CCに替えて, P10, P2tog, RM, TW.

続けてChart 03の18周まで両手共に編む.

周 19(RS): CCでYO, PM, K2tog, MCに替えて, K46 (50, 54, 58), CCに替えて, SSSK.

編み地は返さない. CCを切る. 計48 (52, 56, 60)目.

続けて周20からMCで輪に編み進める.

ミトンは標準の指の長さに合わせてデザインしてあるが, 伸ばす必要がある場合は周20−26の間で必要な周数足せば良い.

周 27–28はS, M, Lのみ編む.

周 29–30はM, Lのみ編む.

周 31–32はLのみ編む.

最終周(XS, Sは50周目, M, Lは51周目)は小さい針で編む. 計12 (16, 16, 20)目.

Kitchener stitch without earsの要領で残りの目をはぐ.

親指

Note: 休めていた15 (15, 17, 17)目の両端の拾い目はゆるみやすいため, ねじりながら拾うとよい.

まず休めていた15 (15, 17, 17)目を針に戻す. 次に糸は付けずにCOとの間から3目拾い, 作り目を解きながら4目, 休み目との間で2目拾う, PM. 計24 (24, 26, 26)目.

MCをつける.

周 1–4: 全ての目をK.

周 5: K15 (15, 17, 17), SSK, Mの2目前までK, K2tog.

周 1–5をあと2回繰り返す. 計18 (18, 20, 20)目.

全ての目をKで13 (15, 17, 17)周し, そのあとK2togを9 (9, 10, 10)回.

糸を切り、残りの目に糸端を通して引き締める.

仕上げ

親指の付け根の穴(もしあれば)を糸端で閉じ, 糸始末する. 仕上がりサイズにピンでブロッキングする.

Chart 01

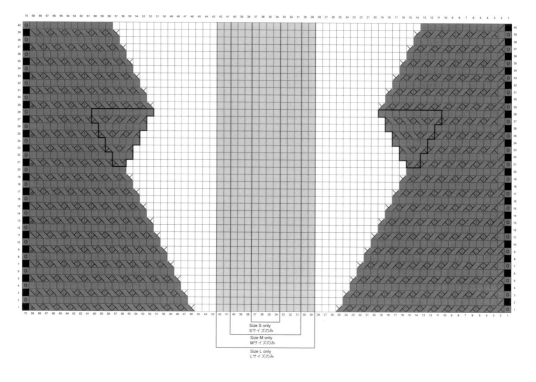

Size S only
Sサイズのみ

Size M only
Mサイズのみ

Size L only
Lサイズのみ

Chart 02 LEFT

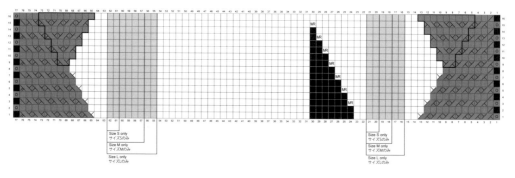

Size S only
サイズのみ

Size M only
サイズMのみ

Size L only
サイズLのみ

Size S only
サイズのみ

Size M only
サイズMのみ

Size L only
サイズLのみ

Chart 02 RIGHT

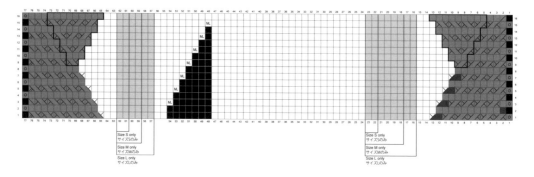

Size S only
サイズのみ

Size M only
サイズMのみ

Size L only
サイズLのみ

Size S only
サイズのみ

Size M only
サイズMのみ

Size L only
サイズLのみ

Size S only
サイズのみ

Size M only
サイズMのみ

Size L only
サイズLのみ

Chart 03

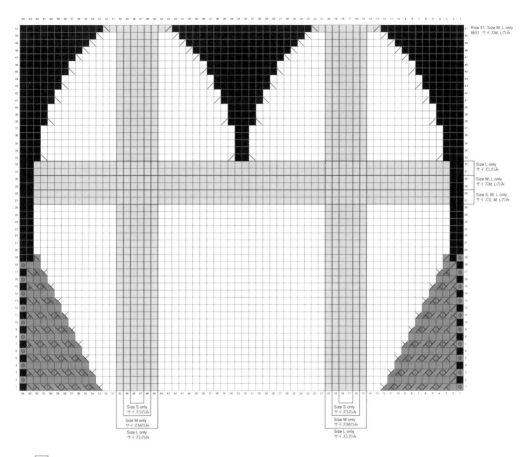

	RS : K, WS : P
O	YO
\	RS : SSK, WS : SSP
/	RS : K2tog, WS : P2tog
|	SSSK
M.	M1L
MR	M1R
	LT2chCC
	RT2chMC
	LT2
	RT2
	LT2togYO
■	no stitch / 目がない
	MC
	CC

Ostinato by Camille Rosselle

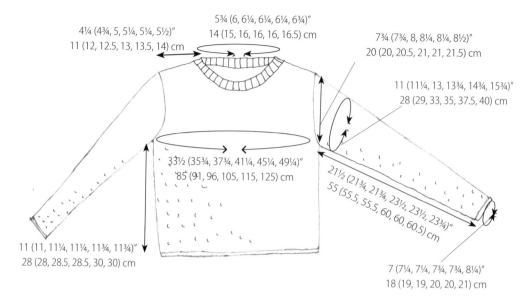

5¾ (6, 6¼, 6¼, 6¼, 6¾)"
14 (15, 16, 16, 16, 16.5) cm

4¼ (4¾, 5, 5¼, 5¼, 5½)"
11 (12, 12.5, 13, 13.5, 14) cm

7¾ (7¾, 8, 8¼, 8¼, 8½)"
20 (20, 20.5, 21, 21, 21.5) cm

11 (11¼, 13, 13¾, 14¾, 15¾)"
28 (29, 33, 35, 37.5, 40) cm

33½ (35¾, 37¾, 41¼, 45¼, 49¼)"
85 (91, 96, 105, 115, 125) cm

21½ (21¾, 21¾, 23½, 23½, 23¾)"
55 (55.5, 55.5, 60, 60, 60.5) cm

11 (11, 11¼, 11¼, 11¾, 11¾)"
28 (28, 28.5, 28.5, 30, 30) cm

7 (7¼, 7¼, 7¾, 7¾, 8¼)"
18 (19, 19, 20, 20, 21) cm

Specifications

Yarn
DK weight yarn

Approximately 1220 (1285, 1400, 1570, 1720, 1880) yards / 1115 (1175, 1315, 1435, 1570, 1720) m

8 (8, 9, 10, 11, 12) balls of DARUMA GENMOU (100% merino wool; 165 yards / 151 m, 50g)

Sample is shown in 13 red

Needles
A US 7 (4.5 mm) 24" / 60 cm (or longer) circular needle

A US 7 (4.5 mm) 16" / 40 cm (or longer) circular needle

A US 6 (4 mm) 16" / 40cm (or longer) circular needle

Or, needles required to obtain gauge

Gauge (after blocking)
24 stitches & 28 rows = 4" / 10 cm in Risotto Stitch with US 7 (4.5 mm) needle

Sizes
Finished chest measurements: XS (S, M, L, XL, XXL) = 33½ (35¾, 37¾, 41¼, 45¼, 49¼)" / 85 (91, 96, 105, 115, 125) cm

The sample was knit in size S with 3½" / 9 cm positive ease.

Tools
Tapestry needle, waste yarn, stitch marker (1 for the collar)

Stitch Guide
Risotto Stitch:

Rows 1 and 3 (RS): K to end.

Row 2 (WS): *P2tog but leave the 2 sts on LH needle, bring yarn to back, K together same 2 sts; repeat from * to end.

Row 4: P1, *P2tog but leave the 2 sts on LH needle, bring yarn to back, K together same 2 sts; repeat from * to last st, P1.

Repeat previous 4 rows.

I-Cord Bind-Off: CO 3 sts and move to LH needle. *K2, SSK, slip 3 sts on LH needle; repeat from * until 4 sts remain on LH needle. BO 1, SSK, BO 1.

Skill Level

Notes
The pullover is knit flat in pieces, starting with a provisional cast on that will be worked later for an I-Cord Bind-Off. Then all pieces are sewn together before picking up stitches for the neckline to be worked in the round. The Risotto Stitch that is used in the pattern is worked by alternating 2 rows. Be sure to work an appropriate row (Row 2 or Row 4) as the count of stitches changes, depending on the decrease or increase, in order to maintain a flow of the Risotto Stitch.

Instruction

BACK

**Using larger needle, Provisionally Cast-On 102 (108, 116, 126, 138, 150) sts.

Work in Risotto Stitch starting with Row 2 until piece measures 11 (11, 11¼, 11¼, 11¾, 11¾)" / 28 (28, 28.5, 28.5, 30, 30) cm. Ending with a WS row.

Armhole Shaping

BO 2 (2, 3, 3, 3, 3) sts at beginning of the next 2 rows and then 0 (0, 0, 0, 0, 2) sts at the beginning of the next 2 rows.

Total of 2 (2, 2, 2, 2, 4) rows have been worked and 98 (104, 110, 120, 132, 140) sts remains.

Size XS (S, M, L, -, -) only

Row 1 (RS): K1, K2tog, K to last 3 sts, SSK, K1.

Row 2 (WS): Work Row 2 or 4 of the Risotto Stitch to maintain the flow of Risotto Stitch.

Repeat previous 2 rows 5 (4, 6, 9, -, -) more times.

Total of 12 (10, 14, 20, -, -) rows have been worked and 86 (94, 96, 100, -, -) sts remains. **

Size - (-, -, -, XL, XXL) only

Row 1 (RS): K1, K2tog, K to last 3 sts, SSK, K1.

Row 2 (WS): P1, SSP, work Row 2 or 4 of the Risotto Stitch to maintain the flow of Risotto Stitch to last 3 sts, P2tog, P1.

Repeat previous 2 rows - (-, -, -, 6, 7) more times and then repeat Row 1 once more.

Total of - (-, -, -, 15, 17) rows have been worked and - (-, -, -, 102, 106) sts remain.*

All Sizes

Continue with the Risotto Stitch until piece measures 7 (7, 7¼, 7½, 7½, 7¾)" / 18 (18, 18.5, 19, 19, 19.5) cm from underarm, ending with a WS row.

Shoulder Shaping using Short Rows

Short Row 1 (RS): K to last 5 sts, turn.

Short Row 2 (WS): Sl1, work Row 2 or 4 of the Risotto Stitch to maintain the flow of Risotto Stitch to last 5 sts, turn.

Short Row 3: Sl1, K to last 10 sts, turn.

Short Row 4: Sl1, work Row 2 or 4 of the Risotto Stitch to maintain the flow of Risotto Stitch to last 10 sts, turn.

Short Row 5: Sl1, K to last 15 sts, turn.

Short Row 6: Sl1, work Row 2 or 4 of the Risotto Stitch to maintain the flow of Risotto Stitch to last 15 sts, turn.

Next row: Sl1, K10 (13, 14, 15, 16, 17), BO 34 (36, 36, 38, 38, 40) sts, break yarn, place the next 26 (29, 30, 31, 32, 33) sts on waste yarn.

With RS facing, place 26 (29, 30, 31, 32, 33) sts of right shoulder on waste yarn.

Carefully undo the provisional cast on and place 102 (108, 116, 126, 138, 150) sts on US 7 (4.5 mm) 24"/ 60 cm needle. Join yarn and use the I-Cord technique to BO.

FRONT

Work as back from ** to ** for sizes XS (S, M, L, -, -) and from ** to * for sizes - (-, -, -, XL, XXL).

Work in the Risotto Stitch until piece measures 3 (2¾, 2¾, 3½, 2, 2½)" / 8 (7, 7, 9, 5, 6.5) cm from underarm, ending with a RS row.

Neckline Shaping

Next row (WS): Work Row 2 or 4 of the Risotto Stitch for 33 (37, 38, 39, 40, 41) sts, place the next 53 (57, 58, 61, 62, 65) sts on waste yarn.

From here, only the right yoke is worked.

Decrease Row (RS): K1, SSK, K to end.

Repeat previous Decrease Row every other row 6 (7, 7, 7, 7, 7) more times, ending with a RS row.

Total of 14 (16, 16, 16, 16, 16) rows have been worked and 26 (29, 30, 31, 32, 33) sts remain.

Work 1 (1, 1, 1, 3, 3) row(s) in Risotto Stitch.

Right Shoulder Shaping with Short Rows

Short Row 1 (RS): K to last 5 sts, turn.

Short Row 2, 4, 6: Sl1, work Row 2 or 4 of the Risotto Stitch to maintain the flow of Risotto Stitch to end.

Short Row 3: K to last 10 sts, turn.

Short Row 5: K to last 15 sts.

Next Row: K to end.

Place the 26 (29, 30, 31, 32, 33) sts on waste yarn. Break yarn leaving a tail long enough for the BO.

Left Yoke of Front Neckline

With WS facing, leave the next 20 (20, 20, 22, 22, 24) sts on waste yarn, put back 33 (37, 38, 39, 40, 41) sts on needles.

Join yarn, work row 2 or 4 of the Risotto Stitch to end.

Decrease Row (RS): K to last 3 sts, K2tog, K1.

Repeat the Decrease Row every other row 6 (7, 7, 7, 7, 7) more times and then work one WS row.

Total of 14 (16, 16, 16, 16, 16) rows have been worked and 26 (29, 30, 31, 32, 33) sts remain.

Work 1 (1, 1, 1, 3, 3) row(s) in Risotto Stitch.

Shoulder Shaping with Short Rows

Short Row 1 (WS): Work Row 2 or 4 of the Risotto Stitch to maintain the flow of Risotto Stitch to last 5 sts, turn.

Short Row 2, 4, 6 (RS): Sl1, K to end.

Short Row 3: Work Row 2 or 4 of the Risotto Stitch to last 10 sts, turn.

Short Row 5: Work Row 2 or 4 of the Risotto Stitch to last 15 sts.

Place 26 (29, 30, 31, 32, 33) sts on waste yarn. Break yarn leaving a long enough tail for the BO.

Carefully undo the provisional cast on and place 102 (108, 116, 126, 138, 150) sts on US 7 (4.5 mm) 24"/ 60 cm needle. Join yarn and use the I-Cord technique to BO.

SLEEVES (both alike)

With the Provisional Cast-On technique, CO 44 (46, 46, 48, 48, 50) sts.

Work 9 (7, 5, 5, 3, 3) rows of the Risotto Stitch beginning with Row 2.

Increase Row (RS): Kfb, K to last 2 sts, Kfb, K1.

Repeat the Increase Row every 10 (8, 6, 6, 4, 4) rows 5 (5, 8, 17, 9, 10) more times and then every 8 (10, 8, 0, 6, 6) rows 6 (6, 8, 0, 11, 12) times.

Work 11 (11, 1, 13, 15, 5) rows in the Risotto Stitch, ending in WS.

Total of 119 (119, 119, 121, 121, 121) rows have been worked, 68 (70, 80, 84, 90, 96) sts remain.

Sleeve Cap Shaping

BO 2 (2, 3, 3, 3, 3) sts at the beginning of the next 2 rows and then 0 (0, 0, 0, 0, 2) sts at the beginning of the next 2 rows. 64 (66, 74, 78, 84, 86) sts remain.

Decrease Row 1 (RS): SSK, K to last 2 sts, K2tog.

Decrease Row 2 (WS): P2tog, work WS of Risotto Stitch to last 2 sts, SSP.

Repeat Dec Row 1 every 2 rows 7 (6, 5, 13, 10, 10) more times and then every row alternating between Dec Rows 1 & 2 when appropriate 18 (20, 24, 18, 24, 24) times.

Total of 34 (34, 36, 46, 46, 46) rows have been worked and 10 (10, 12, 12, 12, 14) sts remain.

Bind-Off.

Carefully undo the provisional cast on and place 44 (46, 46, 48, 48, 50) sts on US 7 (4.5mm) 16"/ 40 cm needle. Join yarn and use the I-Cord technique to BO.

FINISHING

Block pieces to measurements.

Join shoulders using the Three-Needle Bind-Off.

Set in the sleeves carefully easing the sleeve head into position then seam the side and underarm.

NECKLINE

Using 16" circular needles, with RS facing and beginning at left shoulder, attach new yarn, pick up and knit 19 (21, 21, 21, 22, 22) sts from front left neck, place back on needle and knit the 20 (20, 20, 22, 22, 24) sts on waste yarn, pick up and knit 19 (21, 21, 21, 22, 22) sts from front right neck and then 34 (36, 38, 38, 38, 40) sts along back neck. Place a marker for BOR and join to work in the round.

92 (98, 100, 102, 104, 108) sts on needles.

Rib Round: K1, P1.

Continue in ribbing until neckband measures ½" / 1.5 cm from pick up then change to US 6 / 4mm needles. Continue in ribbing until band measures 1 1/4" / 3.5 cm from pick up.

BO in ribbing.

Weave in ends. Wet-block entire garment again if necessary.

詳細情報

Yarn

DK weight yarn.

約 1220 (1285, 1400, 1570, 1720, 1880) yards / 1115 (1175, 1315, 1435, 1570, 1720) m

DARUMA GENMOU (100% merino wool; 165 yards / 151 m, 50g), 8 (8, 9, 10, 11, 12) 玉

サンプル色は13 red

Needles

1 x US 7 (4.5 mm) 24" / 60 cm以上の輪針

1 x US 7 (4.5 mm) 16" / 40 cm以上の輪針

1 x US 6 (4 mm) 16" / 40cm以上の輪針

または、ゲージが取れる太さの針

Gauge (ブロッキング後)

US 7 (4.5 mm) の針を使用し, Risotto Stitchで24目 & 28段 = 10 cm

Sizes

出来上がり寸法: 胸囲 XS (S, M, L, XL, XXL) = 85 (91, 96, 105, 115, 125) cm

モデルはSサイズを着用し, 余裕として+9 cm.

Tools

とじ針, 別糸, 目数マーカー (1, 襟用)

Stitch Guide

Risotto stitch:

段 1と3 (RS): 最後までK.

段 2 (WS): *P2togし, その目を左針に残したまま糸を編地の向こうに持っていき, 同じ2目をK2tog; * からを最後まで繰り返す.

段 4: P1, *P2togし, その目を左針に残したまま糸を編地の向こうに持っていき, 同じ2目をK2tog; * からを最後から1目前まで繰り返す, P1.

段1〜4を繰り返す.

I-Cord Bind-Off: CO 3目. *K2, SSK, 左針に3目を戻す; * からを4目残るまで繰り返す. BO1, SSK, BO1

Skill Level

Note

往復編みで編むプルオーバー. 後から解ける作り目で前後身頃•袖を編んだ後, 作り目を解きI-Cord Bind-Offする. 全体を綴じた後, ネックラインの目を拾い輪で編む. Risotto Stitchは2段を交互に編む. Risotto Stitchの模様を崩さないようにするため, 増目や減目で目数が変わった時には裏側でどちらの段 (段2か段4) を編むのか注意すること

編みかた

後ろ身頃

**後から解ける作り目で, 太い方の針を用いてCO 102 (108, 116, 126, 138, 150)目.

Risotto Stitchを段2から始め, 作り目から28 (28, 28.5, 28.5, 30, 30) cmになるまで編む. WS段で終える.

アームホール

次の2段の始めでBO 2 (2, 3, 3, 3, 3)目, 次の2段の始めでBO 0 (0, 0, 0, 0, 2)目.

計2 (2, 2, 2, 2, 4)段編み終え, 98 (104, 110, 120, 132, 140)目.

XS (S, M, L, -, -)サイズのみ

段 1 (RS): K1, K2tog, 最後から3目前までK, SSK, K1.

段 2 (WS): Risotto Stitchの模様を崩さないように段2または4を編む.

最後の2段をあと5 (4, 6, 9, -, -)回繰り返す.

計12 (10, 14, 20, -, -)段編み終え, 86 (94, 96, 100, -, -)目**

- (-, -, -, XL, XXL) サイズのみ

段 1(RS): K1, K2tog, 最後から3目前までK, SSK, K1.

段 2(WS): P1, SSP, Risotto Stitchの模様を崩さないように段2または4を最後から3目前まで編む, P2tog, P1.

最後の2段をあと - (-, -, -, 6, 7)回繰り返し, 段1をもう一度編む.

計 - (-, -, -, 15, 17)段編み終え, - (-, -, -, 102, 106)目.*

全てのサイズ

Risotto Stitchを続け, 脇から測って18 (18, 18.5, 19, 19, 19.5) cmになるまで編む. WS段で終わる.

引返し編みを使った肩下がり

引返し編み段 1 (RS): 最後の5目前までK, 編地を返す.

引返し編み段 2 (WS): Sl1, Risotto Stitchの模様を崩さないよう段2または4を最後から5目前まで編む, 編地を返す.

引返し編み段 3: Sl1, 最後の10目前までK, 編地を返す.

引返し編み段 4: Sl1, Risotto Stitchの模様を崩さないように段2または4を最後から10目前まで編む, 編地を返す.

引返し編み段 5: Sl1, 最後の15目前までK, 編地を返す.

引返し編み段 6: Sl1, Risotto Stitchの模様を崩さないように段2または4を最後から15目前まで編む, 編地を返す.

次の段: Sl1, K10 (13, 14, 15, 16, 17), BO 34 (36, 36, 38, 38, 40)目, 糸を切り, 次の26 (29, 30, 31, 32, 33)目を別糸に移す.

表側を向けて, 右肩の26 (29, 30, 31, 32, 33)目を別糸に移す.

注意して作り目を解きながら102 (108, 116, 126, 138, 150)目を大きい方の針に移す. 糸をつなぎI-Cord Bind-OffでBO.

前身頃

後ろ身頃と同じように XS (S, M, L, -, -) サイズは**から**まで, - (-, -, -, XL, XXL)サイズは**から*までを編む.

Risotto Stitchでまっすぐに, 脇から測って8 (7, 7, 9, 5, 6.5) cmになるまで編む. RS段で終わる.

ネック減目

次の段(WS): Risotto Stitchesの段2または4を33 (37, 38, 39, 40, 41)目編む, 次の53 (57, 58, 61, 62, 65)目を別糸に移す.

ここから右のヨークを編む.

減目段(RS): K1, SSK, 最後までK.

減目段を2段ごとにあと6 (7, 7, 7, 7, 7)回繰り返す, RS段で終わる.

計14 (16, 16, 16, 16, 16)段編み終え, 26 (29, 30, 31, 32, 33)目.

Risotto Stitchで1 (1, 1, 1, 3, 3)段編む.

引返し編みを使った右肩の肩下がり

引返し編み段 1 (RS): 最後から5目前までK, 編地を返す.

引返し編み段 2, 4, 6 (WS): Sl1, Risotto Stitchの模様を崩さないように段2または4を最後まで編む.

引返し編み段 3: 最後から10目前までK, 編地を返す.

引返し編み段 5: 最後から15目前までK.

次の段: 最後までK.

26 (29, 30, 31, 32, 33)目を別糸に移し, BOに十分な長さを残し糸を切る.

左ヨークのネック減目

編地のWSを見ながら, 次の20 (20, 20, 22, 22, 24)目は別糸に残し, 33 (37, 38, 39, 40, 41)目を針に移す.

糸をつけ, Risotto Stitchの模様を崩さないように段2または4を最後まで編む.

減目段(RS): 最後の3目前までK, K2tog, K1.

減目段を2段ごとにあと6 (7, 7, 7, 7, 7)回繰り返し, WS段を1段編む.

計14 (16, 16, 16, 16, 16)段編み終え, 26 (29, 30, 31, 32, 33)目.
Risotto Stitchで1 (1, 1, 1, 3, 3)段編む.

引返し編みを使った肩下がり

引返し編み段 1 (WS): Risotto Stitchの模様を崩さないように段2または4を最後から5目前まで編む, 編地を返す.

引返し編み段 2, 4, 6 (RS): Sl1, 最後までK.

引返し編み段 3: Risotto Stitchの模様を崩さないように段2または4を最後から10目前まで編む, 編地を返す.

引返し編み段 5: Risotto Stitchの模様を崩さないように段2または4を最後から15目前まで編む.

26 (29, 30, 31, 32, 33)目を別糸に移し, BOに十分な長さを残して糸を切る.

注意して作り目を解き, 102 (108, 116, 126, 138, 150)目を太い方の針に移す. 糸をつなぎ, I-Cord Bind-OffでBO.

袖 (両方とも同じ)

後から解ける作り目で, 太い方の針を用いて, CO 44 (46, 46, 48, 48, 50)目.

Risotto Stitchを段 2 から始めて9 (7, 5, 5, 3, 3)段編む.

増目段(RS): Kfb, 最後から2目前までK, Kfb, K1.

増目段を10 (8, 6, 6, 4, 4)段ごとにあと 5 (5, 8, 17, 9, 10)回, 8 (10, 8, 0, 6, 6)段ごとに6 (6, 8, 0, 11, 12)回繰り返す.

Risotto Stitchを11 (11, 1, 13, 15, 5)段編み, WSで終える.

計119 (119, 119, 121, 121, 121)段編み終え, 68 (70, 80, 84, 90, 96)目.

袖山

次の2段の始めでBO 2 (2, 3, 3, 3, 3)目, 次の2段の始めでBO0 (0, 0, 0, 0, 2)目. 64 (66, 74, 78, 84, 86)目.

減目段 1 (RS): SSK, 最後から2目前までK, K2tog.

減目段 2 (WS): P2tog, Risotto Stitchの段2または4を最後の2目前まで編む, SSP.

減目段1を2段ごとにあと7 (6, 5, 13, 10, 10)回, そのあと減目段1と2を交互に18 (20, 24, 18, 24, 24)回繰り返す.

計34 (34, 36, 46, 46, 46)段編み終え, 10 (10, 12, 12, 12, 14)目.
BO.

注意して作り目を解きながら44 (46, 46, 48, 48, 50)目を大きい方の針に移す. 糸をつなぎ, I-Cord Bind-OffでBO.

仕上げ

完成サイズにブロッキングする.

Three-Needle Bind-Off(引き抜きはぎ)で肩を接ぐ.

袖を身頃に綴じ付け, 袖下と脇を綴じる.

ネックライン

40 cmの太い方の針を用い糸を付け, RSを見ながら左肩から始めて前身頃左ヨークから19 (21, 21, 21, 22, 22)目拾う, 別糸の20 (20, 20, 22, 22, 24)目を針に戻しK, 右ヨークから19 (21, 21, 21, 22, 22)目, 後ろ身頃の首後ろから34 (36, 38, 38, 38, 40)目拾う. BORのマーカーを入れ輪にする.

計92 (98, 100, 102, 104, 108)目.

リブ周: K1, P1.

リブ周をネックバンドが拾い目から1.5 cmになるまで編む. 小さい方の針に替えて拾い目から3.5 cmになるまで編む.

パターン通りに編みながらBO.

糸端を処理し, 必要ならば全体をウェットブロッキングする.

Sunday Market by Ayano Tanaka

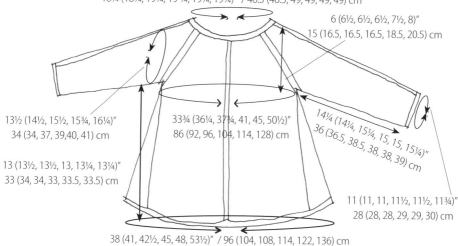

18¼ (18¼, 19¼, 19 ¼, 19¼, 19¼)" / 46.5 (46.5, 49, 49, 49, 49) cm

6 (6½, 6½, 6½, 7½, 8)"
15 (16.5, 16.5, 16.5, 18.5, 20.5) cm

13½ (14½, 15½, 15¾, 16¼)"
34 (34, 37, 39,40, 41) cm

33¾ (36¼, 37¾, 41, 45, 50½)"
86 (92, 96, 104, 114, 128) cm

14¼ (14¼, 15¼, 15, 15, 15¼)"
36 (36.5, 38.5, 38, 38, 39) cm

13 (13½, 13½, 13, 13¼, 13¼)"
33 (34, 34, 33, 33.5, 33.5) cm

11 (11, 11, 11½, 11½, 11¾)"
28 (28, 28, 29, 29, 30) cm

38 (41, 42½, 45, 48, 53½)" / 96 (104, 108, 114, 122, 136) cm

Specifications

Yarn

Worsted weight yarn

Approximately 880 (920, 975, 1060, 1110, 1230) yards, 805 (840, 890, 970, 1015, 1125) m

7 (7, 8, 8, 9, 10) skeins of Quince & Co. Lark (100% American wool; 134 yards / 123 m, 50g)

Sample is shown in 171 (Shell)

Needles

A JP 9 (4.8 mm) 32" / 80 cm circular needle or DPNs

A JP 10 (5.1 mm) 32" / 80 cm circular needle or DPNs

Or , needles required to obtain gauge

Gauge (after blocking)

18 sts & 25 rows = 4" / 10 cm in St st with JP 10 (5.1 mm) needle

Sizes

Finished chest measurement: XS (S, M, L, XL, XXL) = 33¾ (36¼, 37¾, 41, 45, 50½)" / 86 (92, 96, 104, 114, 128) cm

The sample was knit in size S with 4" / 10 cm positive ease.

Tools

Stitch markers (9), tapestry needle, stitch holder or waste yarn, crochet hook for provisional cast on

Stitch Guide

Slip Stitch Knitting Pattern (2 lines in the center of front and back body and each sleeve / 1 line in each side of body):

Rnd (Row) 1: Sl1, K1, Sl1.

Rnd (Row) 2: K or P to end being careful not to twist the slipped st in the previous row.

Decrease (A) (Decrease 2 sts in 2 rounds):

Odd-numbered round: K to 1 st before the 1st M, Sl1, SM, K to the 2nd M, SM, Sl1, K1, Sl1, K to the 3rd M, SM, Sl1, K to 3 sts before the 4th M, K2tog, Sl1, SM, K to the 5th M, SM, Sl1, K1, Sl1, K to the 6th M, SM, Sl1, SSK, K to end.

Even-numbered round: K to end.

Decrease (B) (Decrease 2 sts in 2 rounds):

Odd-numbered round: K to 3 sts before the 1st M, K2tog, Sl1, SM, K to the 2nd M, SM, Sl1, K1, Sl1, K to the 3rd M, SM, Sl1, SSK, K to 1 st before the 4th M, Sl1, SM, K to the 5th M, SM, Sl1, K1, Sl1, K to the 6th M, SM, Sl1, K to end.

Even-numbered round: K to end.

Skill Level

●●○○○

Notes

The body is worked in the round from the bottom up to the underarms. Then, work the front and back separately and set it aside. The sleeves are worked in the round using either the Magic Loop method or DPNs. Then the sleeve caps are worked flat, with the stitches then placed on hold. Once all the pieces are finished, join them together and knit the yoke in the round.

Instruction

Body (front and back)

The Slip Stitch Pattern in the center of the body is worked every 3rd round 4 times, and then worked every other round (row). For side shaping, the Slip Stitch Pattern is worked every other round (row) at each side in both the front and back body, and at the same time, decrease sts to shape A-line.

Using the Chain Cast-On, CO 174 (190, 194, 206, 222, 246) sts using JP 10 (5.1 mm) needle and crochet hook. Join in the round being careful not to twist CO edge.

Rnd 1: PM as BORM, *K6 (8, 8, 8, 9, 9), Sl1, PM, K35 (37, 38, 41, 44, 50), PM, Sl1, K1, Sl1, K35, (37, 38, 41, 44, 50), PM, Sl1, K6 (8, 8, 8, 9, 9); repeat from * once more.

Do not count BORM in. Count from the next M as the 1st M and up to the 6th.

Rnd 2: SM, K to the 2nd M, SM, Sl1, K1, Sl1, K to the 5th M, SM, Sl1, K1, Sl1, K to end.

Rnd 3: SM, K to 1 st before the 1st M, Sl1, SM, K to the 3rd M, SM, Sl1, K to 1 st before the 4th M, Sl1, SM, K to the 6th M, SM, Sl1, K to end.

Rnd 4: Repeat Rnd 2.

Rnd 5: SM, *K to 1 st before M, Sl1, SM, K to next M, SM, Sl1, K1, Sl1, K to next M, SM, Sl1; repeat from * once more, K to end.

Rnd 6: SM, K to end.

Rnd 7: Repeat Rnd 5.

Rnd 8: Repeat Rnd 2.

Rnd 9: SM, K to 3 sts before the 1st M, K2tog, Sl1, SM, K to the 3rd M, SM, Sl1, SSK, K to 1 st before the 4th M, Sl1, SM, K to the 6th M, SM, Sl1, K to end.

Rnd 10: Repeat Rnd 2.

Rnd 11: Repeat Rnd 5.

Rnd 12: K to end.

Rnds 13 - 18: Repeat the last 2 rounds 2 more times, and work Decrease (A). Total 170 (186, 190, 202, 218, 242) sts.

Continuing slip stitch pattern in every other row, decrease body with Decrease (A) & (B).

Sizes XS, S, M, L, XL

*Work even 6 rounds, and work Decrease (B). Work even 6 rounds, and work Decrease (A); repeat from * 2 (0, 3, 2, 2) more times.

Sizes XS, S, L, XL

*Work even 4 rounds, and work Decrease (B). Work even 4 rounds, and work Decrease (A); repeat from * 0 (3, 0, 0) more times.

Size XXL Only

*Work even 8 rounds, and work Decrease (B). Work even 8 rounds, and work Decrease (A); repeat from * 2 more times.

All Sizes

Work 4 (4, 4, 4, 6, 6) rounds as established. Total 154 (166, 174, 186, 202, 230) sts. 13 (13½, 13½, 13, 13¼, 13¼)" / 33 (34, 34, 33, 33.5, 33.5) cm from CO edge.

From this point forward, divide the body into 77 (83, 87, 93, 101, 115) sts each for front and back, and start to work flat.

Front Body

Row 1 (RS): RM, BO 4 (4, 4, 4, 5, 5) sts, K to next M, SM, Sl1, K1, Sl1, K to next M, RM, Sl1, K1 (2, 3, 3, 4, 5).

Size XS Only

Row 2 (WS): BO 4 sts, P to end.

Sizes S, M, L, XL, XXL

Row 2 (WS): BO 4 (4, 4, 5, 5) sts, P to last 3 sts, SSP, P1.

Row 3: K1, SSK, K to M, SM, Sl1, K1, Sl1, K to last 3 sts, K2tog, K1.

Sizes S, M, XL

Row 4: P1, P2tog, P to end.

Size L Only

Row 4: P1, P2tog, P to last 3 sts, SSP, P1.

Row 5: Repeat Row 3.

Row 6: P1, P2tog, P to end.

Size XXL Only

Row 4: P1, P2tog, P to last 3 sts, SSP, P1.

Rows 5, 6: Repeat Rows 3, 4.

Row 7: Repeat Row 3.

Row 8: P1, P2tog, P to end.

All Sizes

Next row: K1, SSK, K to M, SM, Sl1, K1, Sl1, K to last 3 sts, K2tog, K1.

Next row: P to end.

Repeat the last 2 rows 2 (2, 2, 1, 3, 1) more times.

Size XS Only

Work 2 rows as established. Total 63 (65, 69, 73, 79, 89) sts.

End with WS. Transfer the sts to stitch holder or waste yarn without breaking working yarn.

Back Body

Join new yarn and work as for the front body. Cut working yarn, and place the sts on stitch holder or waste yarn.

Sleeves (make two)

CO 51 (51, 51, 53, 53, 55) sts with Chain Cast-On using JP 10 (5.1 mm) needle and crochet hook. Join in the round being careful not to twist CO edge.

Rnd 1: PM as BORM, K24 (24, 24, 25, 25, 26), PM, Sl1, K1, Sl1, K to end.

Rnd 2: SM, K to M, Sl1, K1, Sl1, K to end.

Rnd 3: K to end.

Rnds 4, 5: Repeat Rnd 2.

Rnd 6: K to end.

Rnds 7 - 12: Repeat Rnds 4 - 6, 2 more times.

Rnd 13: Repeat Rnd 2.

Rnd 14: K to end.

Rnd 15 - : Repeat the last 2 rounds 15 (15, 16, 17, 17, 18) more times. Piece measures 7 (7, 7¼, 7½, 7½, 7¾)" / 17.5 (17.5, 18.5, 19, 19, 20) cm.

Sleeve Increases

Next Rnd (Increase Rnd): SM, K1, M1L, K to M, SM, Sl1, K1, Sl1, K to 1 st before M, M1R, K1.

Continuing Slip Stitch Knitting Pattern in every other round, work Increase Rnd every 10 (10, 6, 6, 6, 6) th round 4 (4, 7, 5, 4, 4) more times.

Sizes L, XL, XXL

Work Increase Rnd every 4th round 3 (5, 5) more times.

All Sizes

Work 5 (7, 7, 5, 3, 3) rounds as established. Total 61 (61, 67, 71, 73, 75) sts.

14¼ (14½, 15¼, 15, 15, 15¼)" / 36 (36.5, 38.5, 38, 38, 39) cm from CO edge.

From this point forward, start working flat.

Row 1 (RS): RM, BO 4 (4, 4, 4, 5, 5) sts, K to M, SM, Sl1, K1, Sl1, K to end.

Row 2 (WS): BO 4 (4, 4, 4, 5, 5) sts, P to end.

Row 3: K1, SSK, K to M, SM, Sl1, K1, Sl1, K to last 3 sts, K2tog, K1.

Row 4: P to end.

Repeat the last 2 rows 3 (2, 3, 4, 3, 3) more times.

Work 0 (2, 0, 0, 2, 2) more rows as established. Total 45 (47, 51, 53, 55, 57) sts.

Break working yarn, and place sts on stitch holder or waste yarn.

Yoke (raglan decrease)

PM for raglan, and place the stitches on hold for the front and back body and sleeves on needle.

Set up round: PM as BORM, 63 (65, 69, 73, 79, 89) sts for front body, PM, 45 (47, 51, 53, 55, 57) sts for right sleeve, PM, 63 (65, 69, 73, 79, 89) sts for back body, PM, 45 (47, 51, 53, 55, 57) sts for left sleeve. Total 216 (224, 240, 252, 268, 292) sts.

As BOR, start from front body with yarn attached, and work in the round.

Continue working as established, and at the same time, decrease sts on both sides of each raglan line in both front and back body, total 8 times decreases across a round.

Sizes XS, S, L, XL, XXL

Rnd 1: Work to end as established.

Rnd 2: *K1, SSK, K to 3 sts before next raglan M, K2tog, K1, SM, K to M; repeat from * once more.

Sizes XS, S, M

Work 2 rounds as established.

Decrease Rnd: K1, SSK, *K to 3 sts before next raglan M, K2tog, K1, SM, K1, SSK; repeat from * 2 more times. K to 3 sts before M, K2tog, K1.

Work Decrease Rnd every 3rd round 3 (3, 1) more times.

All Sizes

Next Rnd: Work to end as established.

Decrease Rnd: K1, SSK, *K to 3 sts before next raglan M, K2tog, K1, SM, K1, SSK; repeat from * 2 more times. K to 3 sts before M, K2tog, K1.

Work Decrease Rnd in every other round 11 (12, 16, 17, 19, 22) more times.

Sizes L, XL, XXL

Repeat Decrease Rnd 2 more times. Total 84 (84, 88, 88, 88, 88) sts.

Collar

Change to JP 9 (4.8mm) needle.

Continue working 11 rounds or 2¼" / 5.5 cm as established.

Fold the collar inward in half, and BO loosely by K2tog with corresponding loops in the last raglan decrease round and sts on needle.

Seam the sides.

Finishing

Keeping the curl of hem, block to measurements.

詳細情報

Yarn

Worsted weight yarn

約880 (920, 975, 1060, 1110, 1230) yards, 805 (840, 890, 970, 1015, 1125) m

Quince & Co. Lark (100% American wool; 134 yards / 123 m, 50g), 7 (7, 8, 8, 9, 10) カセ

サンプル色は171 (Shell)

Needles

1 x JP 9 (4.8 mm) 32" / 80 cmの輪針もしくは4本棒針

1 x JP 10 (5.1 mm) 32" / 80 cmの輪針もしくは4本棒針

または、ゲージに合わせた太さの針

Gauge (ブロッキング後)

JP 10 (5.1 mm)の針を使用し, メリヤス編みで18目 & 25段 = 10 cm

Sizes

出来上がり寸法: 胸囲XS (S, M, L, XL, XXL) = 86 (92, 96, 104, 114, 128) cm

モデルはSサイズを着用し, 余裕として+10 cm.

Tools

目数マーカー (9), 綴じ針, ステッチホルダー又は別糸, 作り目用のかぎ針1本

Stitch Guide

引き上げ模様 (前後身頃中央, 袖それぞれ2本ずつ / 脇1本):

周(段) 1: Sl1, K1, Sl1.

周(段) 2: 前段のすべり目をねじらないように, すべてKまたはP.

減目(A) (2周で2目減目する):

奇数周: 1番目のMの1目前までK, Sl1, SM, 2番目のMまでK, SM, Sl1, K1, Sl1, 3番目のMまでK, SM, Sl1, 4番目のMの3目前までK, K2tog, Sl1, SM, 5番目のMまでK, SM, Sl1, K1, Sl1, 6番目のMまでK, SM, Sl1, SSK, 段の最後までK.

偶数周: すべてK.

減目(B) (2周で2目減目する):

奇数周: 1番目のMの3目前までK, K2tog, Sl1, SM, 2番目のMまでK, SM, Sl1, K1, Sl1, 3番目のMまでK, SM, Sl1, SSK, 4番目のMの1目前までK, Sl1, SM, 5番目のMまでK, SM, Sl1, K1, Sl1, 6番目のMまでK, SM, Sl1, 段の最後までK.

偶数周: すべてK.

Skill Level

●●○○○

Note

前後身頃は裾から上に向かって輪で編み進める. 脇下まで編んだら前後身頃を分けて編み, 目を休めておく. 袖はマジックループまたは4本棒針で輪で編み始め, 袖山からは往復編みで編み, 目を休める. 全てのパーツが編み終わったら, 各パーツをつなげてヨークを輪で編む.

編みかた

前後身頃

身頃中央の引き上げ編みは3段ごと1模様を4回編んだ後, 2段ごと1模様を編んでいく. 両脇は各2か所の計4ヶ所で2段ごとの引き上げ編みを編むと同時にAラインの減目をしていく.

JP10号の針とかぎ針を使い, Chain cast onでCO 174 (190, 194, 206, 222, 246)目, ねじらないように気をつけて輪にする.

周1: BORMとしてPM, *K6 (8, 8, 8, 9, 9), SI1, PM, K35 (37, 38, 41, 44, 50), PM, SI1, K1, K35, (37, 38, 41, 44, 50), PM, SI1, K6 (8, 8, 8, 9, 9), *以降をあと1回編む.

BORMは数えず, 次のMから1番目～6番目と数える.

周2: SM, 2番目のMまでK, SM, SI1, K1, SI1, 5番目のMまでK, SM, SI1, K1, SI1, 周の最後までK.

周3: SM, 1番目のMの1目前までK, SI1, SM, 3番目のMまでK, SM, SI1, 4番目のMの1目前までK, SI1, SM, 6番目のMまでK, SM, SI1, 周の最後までK.

周4: 周2を編む.

周5: SM, *Mの1目前までK, SI1, SM, 次のMまでK, SM, SI1, K1, SI1, 次のMまでK, SM, SI1, *以降をあと1回編む, 周の最後までK.

周6: SM, すべてK.

周7: 周5を編む.

周8: 周2を編む.

周9: SM, 1番目のMの3目前までK, K2tog, SI1, SM, 3番目のMまでK, SM, SI1, SSK, 4番目のMの1目前までK, SI1, SM, 6番目のMまでK, SM, SI1, 周の最後までK.

周10: 周2を編む.

周11: 周5を編む.

周12: すべてK.

周13～18: 最後の2周をあと2回編み, 減目(A)を編む. 計170 (186, 190, 202, 218, 242)目.

引き続きパターン通りに2段ごとにすべり目の引き上げ模様を編みながら, 身頃の減目(A) & (B)をしていく.

XS, S, M, L, XLサイズのみ

*6周編み, 減目(B)を編む. 6周編み, 減目(A)を編む, *以降をあと2 (0, 3, 2, 2)回編む.

XS, S, L, XLサイズのみ

*4周編み, 減目(B)を編む. 4周編み, 減目(A)を編む, *以降をあと0 (3, 0, 0)回編む.

XXLサイズのみ

*8周編み, 減目(B)を編む. 8周編み, 減目(A)を編む, *以降をあと2回編む.

全サイズ

4 (4, 4, 4, 6, 6)周パターン通りに編む. 計154 (166, 174, 186, 202, 230)目. 作り目から33 (34, 34, 33, 33.5, 33.5) cm.

ここより前後身頃を77 (83, 87, 93, 101, 115)目ずつに分けて, 往復編みで編む.

前身頃

段1 (RS): RM, BO 4 (4, 4, 4, 5, 5)目, 次のMまでK, SM, SI1, K1, SI1, 次のMまでK, RM, SI1, K1 (2, 3, 3, 4, 5).

XSサイズのみ

段2 (WS): BO 4目, 最後までP.

S, M, L, XL, XXLサイズのみ

段2 (WS): BO 4 (4, 4, 5, 5)目, 最後の3目前までP, SSP, P1.

段3: K1, SSK, MまでK, SM, SI1, K1, SI1, 段の最後の3目前までK, K2tog, K1.

S, M, XLサイズのみ

段4: P1, P2tog, 最後までP.

Lサイズのみ

段4: P1, P2tog, 最後の3目前までP, SSP, P1.

段5: 段3を編む.

段6: P1, P2tog, 最後までP.

XXLサイズのみ

段4: P1, P2tog, 最後の3目前までP, SSP, P1.

段5, 6: 段3, 4を編む.

段7: 段3を編む.

段8: P1, P2tog, 最後までP.

全サイズ

次の段: K1, SSK, MまでK, SM, SI1, K1, SI1, 最後の3目前までK, K2tog, K1.

次の段: すべてP.

最後の2段をあと2 (2, 2, 1, 3, 1)回編む.

XSサイズのみ

パターン通りに2段編む. 計63 (65, 69, 73, 79, 89)目.

編み終わりはWS段, 糸玉は切らずにステッチホルダー又は別糸に目を休ませておく.

後ろ身頃

後ろ身頃に新しい糸をつけて, 前身頃と同様に編む. 糸を切り, ステッチホルダー又は別糸に休ませる.

袖 (2枚編む)

JP10号の針とかぎ針を使い, Chain cast onでCO 51 (51, 51, 53, 53, 55)目, ねじらないように気をつけて輪にする.

周1: BORMとしてPM, K24 (24, 24, 25, 25, 26), PM, SI1, K1, SI1, 周の最後までK.

周2: SM, MまでK, SI1, K1, SI1, 最後までK.

周3: すべてK.

周4, 5: 周2を編む.

周6: すべてK.

周7 - 12: 周4 - 6をあと2回編む.

周13: 周2を編む.

周14: すべてK.

周15 - : 最後の2周をあと15 (15, 16, 17, 17, 18)回編む.

17.5 (17.5, 18.5, 19, 19, 20) cm.

袖の増目

次の周 (増目周): SM, K1, M1L, MまでK, SM, SI1, K1, SI1, M
の1目前までK, M1R, K1.

パターン通りに2段ごとにすべり目の模様を編みながら, 10 (10, 6, 6, 6, 6)周ごとに増目周1回をあと4 (4, 7, 5, 4, 4)回編む.

L, XL, XXLサイズのみ

パターン通りに4周ごとに増目周1回をあと3 (5, 5)回編む.

全サイズ

パターン通りに5 (7, 7, 5, 3, 3) 周編む. 計61 (61, 67, 71, 73, 75)目.

作り目から36 (36.5, 38.5, 38, 38, 39) cm.

ここから往復編みで編む.

段1 (RS): RM, BO 4 (4, 4, 4, 5, 5)目, MまでK, SM, SI1, K1, SI1, 最後までK.

段2 (WS): BO 4 (4, 4, 4, 5, 5)目, 最後までP.

段3: K1, SSK, MまでK, SM, SI1, K1, SI1, 最後から3目前までK, K2tog, K1.

段4: すべてP.

最後の2段をあと3, (2, 3, 4, 3, 3)回編む.

パターン通りにあと0 (2, 0, 0, 2, 2)段編む. 計45 (47, 51, 53, 55, 57)目.

糸を切り, ステッチホルダー又は別糸に目を休ませておく.

ヨーク (ラグランの減目)

ラグラン用のMを付けながら, 前後身頃と袖の休み目を針に戻す.

セットアップ周: BORMとしてPM, 前身頃63 (65, 69, 73, 79, 89)目, PM, 右袖45 (47, 51, 53, 55, 57)目, PM, 後ろ身頃63 (65, 69, 73, 79, 89)目, PM, 左袖45 (47, 51, 53, 55, 57)目. 合計216 (224, 240, 252, 268, 292)目.

糸玉がついている前身頃を周の始まりとし, 輪で編んでいく.

パターン通りに編みながら, 同時にラグラン線の両サイド 2 ヶ所の計8 ヶ所で減目をしていく.

XS, S, L, XL, XXLサイズのみ

周1: パターン通りに1周編む.

周2: *K1, SSK, 次のラグランMの3目前までK, K2tog, K1, SM, 次のMまでK, *以降をあと1回編む.

XS, S, Mサイズのみ

パターン通りに2周編む.

減目周: K1, SSK, *次のラグランMの3目前までK, K2tog, K1, SM, K1, SSK, *以降をあと2回編む. Mの3目前までK, K2tog, K1.

3周ごとに減目周1回を, あと3 (3, 1)回編む.

全サイズ

次の周: パターン通りに1周編む.

減目周: K1, SSK, *次のラグランMの3目前までK, K2tog, K1, SM, K1, SSK, *以降をあと2回編む. Mの3目前までK, K2tog, K1.

2周ごとに減目周1周を, あと11 (12, 16, 17, 19, 22)回編む.

L, XL, XXLサイズのみ

減目周を2回編む. 計84 (84, 88, 88, 88, 88)目.

襟

JP 9の針に替える.

引き続きパターン通りに11周または5.5 cm編む.

襟を内側にふたつに折り, ラグランラインの最後の減目周のループと針の目をK2togしながら, ゆるめにBO.
両脇を綴じる.

仕上げ

裾のカールを崩さないようにブロッキングする.

Raindrops by Mizuho Komiya

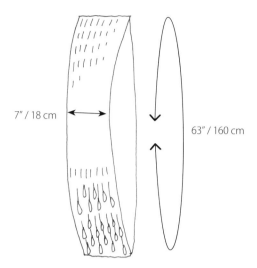

7" / 18 cm

63" / 160 cm

Specifications

Yarn

Fingering weight yarn

(C1) Approximately 525 yards, 480 m

(C2) Approximately 525 yards, 480 m

Hedgehog Fibres Skinny Singles (100 % merino wool; 400 yards / 366 m, 100g)

Sample is shown in (C1) Salty Dales (2 skeins) and (C2) Pucker (2 skeins)

Needles

A US 3 (3.25 mm) 32" / 80 cm (or longer) circular needle

A US 5 (3.75 mm) 32" / 80 cm (or longer) circular needle

A smaller circular needle than US 3 (for grafting)

Or, needles required to obtain gauge

Gauge (after blocking)

30 stitches & 28 rows = 4" / 10 cm in stranded pattern with US 5 (3.75 mm)

30 stitches & 32 rows = 4" / 10 cm in St st with US 3 (3.25 mm)

Size

Finished measurements: circumference 63" / 160 cm, height 7" / 18 cm

Tools

Stitch marker (1), waste yarn(4 - 5 yards / 4 - 5 m, for CO), tapestry needle, JP 3 (2.3mm) crochet hook for CO

Skill Level

Notes

A doughnut shaped cowl that is worked in the round using the Magic Loop method, starting with a provisional CO and finishing in grafting stitches from the beginning and the end using Kitchener stitch. The first half is knitted in two colors while the second half is worked in an opposite color scheme.

Instruction

Using the Crocheted Provisional Cast-On method, waste yarn, and a crochet hook, CO 108 sts in C1 on smaller needle.

In C1 K all sts. PM for BOR and join in the round.

K 19 rounds.

Chart A

Rnd 1(RS): Change to larger needle and attach C2, work Rnd 1 of Chart A, repeating inside of square 7 more times after the first 24 sts.

Rnds 2 – 65: Work Chart A.

Chart B

Rnd 1: Repeat Rnd 1 of Chart B to end.

Rnds 2 – 8: Work Chart B.

Repeat Rnds 1- 8 15 more times.

In C1, K 3 rounds.

Chart C

Rnd 1: Repeat Rnd 1 of Chart C to end.

Rnds 2 - 6: Work Chart C.

Break C1.

(Swap colors from here)

Change to smaller needle, in C2, K 25 rounds.

Chart A

Rnd 1: Change to larger needle and attach C1, work Rnd 1 of Chart A using C1 and C2, repeating inside of square 7 more times after the first 24 sts. Make sure to use opposite colors to the first half.

Rnds 2 – 65: Work Chart A.

Chart B

Rnd 1: Work Rnd 1 of Chart B to end, making sure to use opposite colors to the first half.

Rnds 2 – 8: Work Chart B.

Repeat Rnds 1 - 8 15 more times.

In C2, K 3 rounds.

Chart C

Rnd 1: Work Rnd 1 of Chart C to end, making sure to use opposite colors to the first half.

Rnds 2 – 6: Work Chart C.

Change to smaller needle, in C1, K 5 rounds.

Turn WS out and weave ends in. Then turn RS out.

Unravel CO and transfer sts on a needle smaller than US3. (108 sts).

Using Kitchener stitch, graft the sts from RS, making sure that the pattern at each end aligns.

Finishing

Lightly block and iron.

詳細情報

Yarn

Fingering weight yarn

(C1) 約480 m

(C2) 約480 m

Hedgehog Fibres Skinny Singles (100 % merino wool; 約 400 yards / 366 m, 100g)

サンプル色は(C1) Salty Dales 2カセ, (C2) Pucker 2カセ

Needles

1 x US 3 (3.25 mm) 32″ / 80 cm (またはそれ以上の長さ)の 輪針

1 x US 5 (3.75 mm) 32″ / 80 cm (またはそれ以上の長さ)の 輪針

JP3号かぎ針 (作り目用)

US3号より細い輪針 (メリヤスはぎ用)

Gauge (ブロッキング後)

US 5 (3.75 mm)の針を使用し, 模様編みで約30目 & 28段 = 10 cm

US 3 (3.25 mm)の針を使用し、メリヤス編みで約30目 & 32段 = 10 cm

Size

出来上がり寸法 (長さ): 円周160 cm, 高さ18 cm

Tools

目数マーカー (1), 別糸4 - 5 m (作り目用), JP3号かぎ針 (作 り目用)

Skill Level

Note

ドーナツのような形のカウル.

後でほどける作り目で作り目し, マジックループを使って 輪で編み進める. 中間地点でC1とC2の配色を反転させ残 りの半分を編む.

最後に, 作り目をほどいて拾った目と編み終わりの周の目 を合わせてメリヤスはぎで綴じる.

編みかた

別糸と3号かぎ針を使い, 後でほどける作り目 (Crocheted provisional cast on)で細い方の針にCO108目.

C1で1段K, 編み始めにMをいれ、ねじれないように輪にし て19周K.

チャートAを編む

周1: 太い方の針に替えてC2を付け, チャートAの周1を編 む. 25目以降は太枠部分を周の最後まであと7回繰り返す.

周2 – 65: チャートAを編む.

チャートBを編む

周1: チャートBの周1を最後まで繰り返す.

周2 - 8: チャートBを編む.

周 1 - 8をあと15回編む.

C1で3周K.

チャートCを編む

周1: チャートCの周1を最後まで繰り返す.

周2 – 6: チャートCを編む.

C1を切る.

(ここからC1とC2の配色を入れ替える)

細い方の針に替えてC2で25周K.

チャートAを編む

周1: 太い方の針に替えてC1を付け, 1回目と配色を逆にし てチャートAの周1を編む. 25目以降は太枠部分を周の最後 まであと7回繰り返す.

周2 – 65: チャートAを編む.

チャートBを編む

周1: チャートBの周1を, 1回目と配色を逆にして最後まで 繰り返す.

周2 - 8: チャートBを編む.

周1 - 8をあと15回編む.

C2で3周K.

チャートCを編む

周1: チャートCの周1を, 1回目と配色を逆にして最後まで 繰り返す.

周2 - 6: チャートCを編む.

細い方の針に替えて, C1で5周K.

編地を裏返し, 糸の始末をした後, 編地を外表に戻す.

作り目の別糸をほどき, US3号より細い号数の輪針に目を 移す. (108目).

編み始めの周と編み終わりの周の位置がずれないように 気をつけて, RSを見ながらメリヤスはぎをする.

仕上げ

軽くブロッキングをしてアイロンをかける.

Chart A

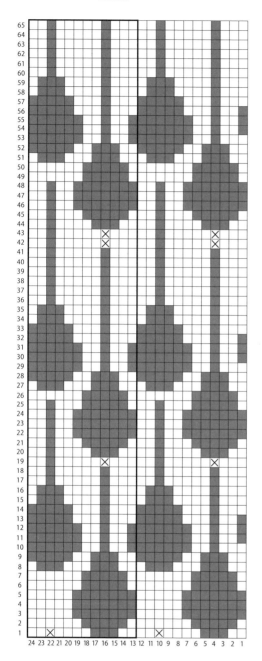

Chart B

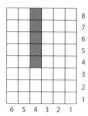

Chart C

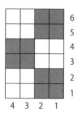

☐ C1 (1st time), C2 (2nd time) / C1 (1回目), C2 (2回目)

■ C2 (1st time), C1 (2nd time) / C2 (1回目), C1 (2回目)

☒ Weave CC
編地の裏側で渡り糸のCCとMCの糸をクロスさせる.

Abbreviations / Pattern Notes

K	Knit	表目	psso	Pass slipped stitch over	すべらせた目に被せる
P	Purl	裏目	Sl	Slip stitch	すべり目
K tbl	Knit through back of loop	表のねじり目	Sl wyb	Slip st with yarn in back	すべり目
RS	Right Side	表面	Sl wyf	Slip st with yarn in front	浮き目
WS	Wrong Side	裏面	YO	Yarn over	掛け目
CO	Cast On	作り目	Kfb	Knit (Purl) into front & back of st	目の前と後ろのループにK(P)を編み入れる
BO	Bind Off	伏せ目	K2tog	Knit 2 together	左上2目一度
BOR	Beginning of round	段の開始位置	K2tog tbl	Knit 2 together through the back loop	左上2目一度(ねじり目)
CN	Cable needle	縄編み針	SSK	Slip 2 stitches as if to knit, knit them together through the back loops	右上2目一度
MC	Main color	地色			
CC	Contrasting color	配色糸			
M	Marker	マーカー	P2tog	Purl 2 sts together	裏左上2目一度
PM	Place Marker	マーカーを入れる	SSP	Slip 2 stitches as if to K. Slip the two slipped stitches back to the left needle. Then purl them together through the back loops.	裏右上2目一度
SM	Slip Marker	マーカーを移す			
RM	Remove Marker	マーカーを外す			
St st	Stockinette stitch	メリヤス編み			
Rnd	round	周			
TW	Turn work	編地を裏返す	SSSK	Slip slip slip knit (double decrease)	右上3目一度
RH	Right Hand	右手	S2KP	Slip 2, knit 1 pass slipped sts over Slip, k2tog, psso	中上3目一度
LH	Left Hand	左手			
st(s)	Stitch(es)	編み目	K3tog	Knit 3 together	左上3目一度
DPN	Double pointed needles	4本棒針			

Backward loop cast on

Step 1: Begin with a slipknot and take your knitting needle and the tail of your yarn in your dominant hand.

Step 2: Grab your yarn with your other hand and stretch it out a few inches from your needle.

Step 3: Take your index finger and wrap the yarn around it. You can use your thumb instead if you prefer.

Step 4: Begin by going over the top, to under, and then around to the top again. You should now have a loop on your finger.

Step 5: Slide your knitting needle into the side of the loop, next to your finger.

Step 6: Pull your finger out of the loop and tighten the yarn onto the needle.

Repeat steps 2 - 6 until you have cast on the number of stitches required by the pattern.

Long tail tubular CO for 1x1 rib

Make a slip knot loop and place it on the needle (counts as first st CO), leaving a tail approx. 3 times longer than the width of the piece to be cast on. Hold needle in right hand with the tail to the back and the ball end of the yarn to the front. Slip left thumb and index finger between the strands, so that ball yarn goes from the needle over

Long tail tubular cast on(一目ゴム編みの作り目)

出来上がり幅の3倍の長さの糸を残して, 引き結びで1目作り, 編み針に置く.(この目を1目と数える) 指で掛ける作り目をするように, 針を右手に持ち, 糸端を向こう, 糸玉を手前にし, 人差し指と親指に糸を掛ける.

ステップ1: 針先を2本の糸の後ろ側から下へ持ってくる. 親指側の糸にループを1つ作るように2本の糸の間を前から後ろに引っ掛けて, 2本の糸の後ろ側から持ち上げる(裏目の作り目1目).

ステップ2: 針先を親指の下から入れて, 1ループを作るように2本の糸の間から人差し指の方の糸を前から後ろに向かって糸を掛け, 両方の糸の後ろ側から前に持ってくる(表目の作り目1目).

ステップ1と2を必要な目数になるまで繰り返す.

Crochet Provisional Cast On (Provisional Cast on)

後から解ける作り目

Crochet Chain Cast On

かぎ針にスリップノットを作る. 棒針と編み糸を左手にかぎ針を右手に持ち, 編み糸を棒針の下に持ってく. 棒針に糸を巻き付けるように上側からかぎ針に糸を掛けて引き抜く. *糸を棒針の下側に戻して, 上から棒針に糸を巻き付

the top of your thumb, and the tail goes from the needle over the top of your index finger; hold the ends against your palm, just as for working an ordinary long-tail CO.

Step 1: Put the tip of the needle over, then underneath both strands from behind. Put the needle over the thumb strand only, hooking it so that 1 loop is added to the needle, then bring needle to back under both strands (1 purl st CO).

Step 2: Put the tip of the needle under the thumb strand, over the index finger strand, then bring it back under both strands to the front, so that 1 loop is added to the needle (1 knit st CO).

Repeat Steps 1 and 2 until required number of sts are cast on.

As you CO, make sure that you keep the loops over the top of the needle, and the twists and nubs running along the underside of the needle.

Crochet Provisional Cast On (Provisional Cast On)

1. With waste yarn and crochet hook, crochet chains loosely. At that time, crochet several chains longer than the required number of CO stitches. Break yarn and pull the tail through the last loop.

2. Insert knitting needle into a bump on the back of the last chain and pull the main yarn in the same way to knit. Continue until reaching the required number of CO sts.

3. When you pick up stitches, undo the chains by pulling out the waste yarn and transfer the stitches onto needle.

Crochet Chain Cast On

Place a slipknot on crochet hook. Hold knitting needle and yarn in your left hand and hook in your right hand, with yarn under needle. Place hook over needle, wrap yarn around hook and pull loop through loop on hook. *Bring yarn to back under needle, wrap yarn around hook, and pull it through loop on hook. Repeat from * until there is one fewer than the desired number of stitches on needle. Slip loop from hook to needle for last stitch.

Three needle bind off (3-needle cast off)

Have the pieces to be joined on separate needles, hold together in the left hand with the wrong sides facing each other. Using a spare needle and yarn tail, insert right needle into first st on front needle, then first st on back needle and K2tog. *Insert right needle into next st on front needle, then next st on back needle and k2tog. Pass first st on right needle over second st to BO 1 st. Rep from *.

けるようにかぎ針に糸を掛けて引き抜く. 必要な目より1目少ない目数になるまで*以降を繰り返す. 最後の目はかぎ針に掛かっている目を棒針に移す.

Three needle bind off

引き抜きはぎ

Tubular BO

一目ゴム編み止め

Garter stitch

ガーター編み
段1 (RS): 全ての目をK.
段2 (WS): 全ての目をK.
段1, 2を繰り返す.

M1L, M1 (M1PL, M1LP) & M1R (M1PR, M1RP)

M1L, M1 (M1PL, M1LP): 目と目の間に渡っている糸(シンカーループ)を左針で手前側からすくう. このすくった目をねじり表編み(裏編み)する. 1目増目.

M1R (M1PR, M1RP): 目と目の間に渡っている糸 (シンカーループ)を左針で後ろ側からすくう. このすくった目をねじり表編み(裏編み)する. この時, 目の向きが通常と異なっているため, 針は手前から差し込む. 1目増目.

W&T (Wrap & Turn)

表側でのW&T: パターン内でW&Tの場所にきたら, 糸を手前に持っていき, 次の目を右針にすべり目. 手前に持ってきた糸をすべった目の左から回すように後ろに持っていき, すべった目をまた左針に戻す. 編地を返し, そのまま編み進める.

裏側でのW&T: パターン内でW&Tの場所にきたら, 糸を向こう側に持っていき, 次の目を右針にすべり目. 向こう側に持っていった糸をすべった目の左から回すように手前に持っていき, すべった目を また左針に戻す. 編地を返し, そのまま編み進める.

段消し
表側での段消し: ラップされた目の手前まで編む. ラップされた目を右針へ移し, 左針を使って目の下に巻き付いた目を取る. この2目を2目一度する.

裏側での段消し: ラップされた目の手前まで編む. ラップされた目を右針へ移し, 左針を使って目の下に巻き付いた目を取る. この2目をねじり目の裏2目一度する.

Tubular BO for 1x1 rib

Cut yarn leaving a tail approx. 3 times the width of the piece to be bound off. Thread the tail on a tapestry needle. These instructions assume the row/round begins with k1.

Step 1: Insert tapestry needle into first st on knitting needle purlwise and pull yarn through.

Step 2: With tapestry needle behind the work, insert it knitwise into first purl st on knitting needle and pull yarn through.

Step 3: Insert tapestry needle into first knit st knitwise but do not pull yarn through, drop st from knitting needle. Insert tapestry needle purlwise into next knit st and pull yarn through.

Step 4: Insert tapestry purlwise into first purl st but do not pull yarn through, drop st from knitting needle. With tapestry needle behind the work, insert it knitwise into next purl st and pull yarn through.

Repeat steps 3 and 4 until all sts are bound off.

Garter stitch

Row 1 (RS): K all sts.
Row 2 (WS): K all sts.
Repeat Rows 1 & 2.

M1L, M1 (M1PL, M1LP) & M1R (M1PR, M1RP)

M1L, M1 (M1PL, M1LP): Insert left needle, from front to back, under strand of yarn which runs between next stitch on left needle and last stitch on right needle; knit (purl) this stitch through back loop. 1 stitch increased.

Kitchener stitch

1. Bring tapestry needle through front stitch as if to purl and leave stitch on needle.

2. Bring tapestry needle through back stitch as if to purl and leave stitch on needle.

3. Bring tapestry needle through first front stitch as if to knit and slip this stitch off needle. Bring tapestry needle through next front stitch as if to purl and leave stitch on needle.

4. Bring tapestry needle through first back stitch as if to knit and slip this stitch off, bring needle through next back stitch as if to purl, leave this stitch on needle.

Repeat Steps 3 & 4 until all sts are worked.

Magic Loop (マジックループ)

長い輪針で小さな輪を編む技法。この技法を使うには、柔らかいコードの輪針が必要となる。まず輪針に掛かっている目を均等に分け、目と目の間からコードを引き出す。両針が右側にくるように揃えて持ち、後ろ側の針を引っ張ってコードを引き出す。その針を使って手前の針に掛かっている目を編んでいく。編み終わった後は、編地を返し、コードを引っ張って手前の針先に目がくるようにする。これを繰返し輪編みする。

Mattress stitch

すくい綴じ

Kitchener stitch

1. 手前の針に掛かっている目に綴じ針を裏を編むように入れる。目は針から抜かない。

2. 奥の針に掛かっている目に綴じ針を裏を編むように入れる。目は針から抜かない。

3. 手前の針に掛かっている最初の目に表を編むように綴じ針を入れ、目を針から落とす。針から落とした目の隣の目に裏を編むように綴じ針を入れる。目は針から抜かない。

4. 奥の針に掛かっている最初の目に表を編むように綴じ針を入れ、目を針から落とし、その目の隣の目に裏を編むように綴じ針を入れ、その目は針に残す。

このステップ3・4を目がなくなるまで繰り返す。

Three Diamonds Bag

Specifications

Yarn: DARUMA Lace #20   (A) Olive (11) 100 g (2 balls)

                         (B) Beige (3) 75 g (2 balls), Black (15) 25 g (1 ball)

Crochet Hook: 2.0 mm

Gauge: 31 sts x 37 rows = 4" / 10 cm in sc

Finished Measurement: 24 cm in width, 18 cm in hight

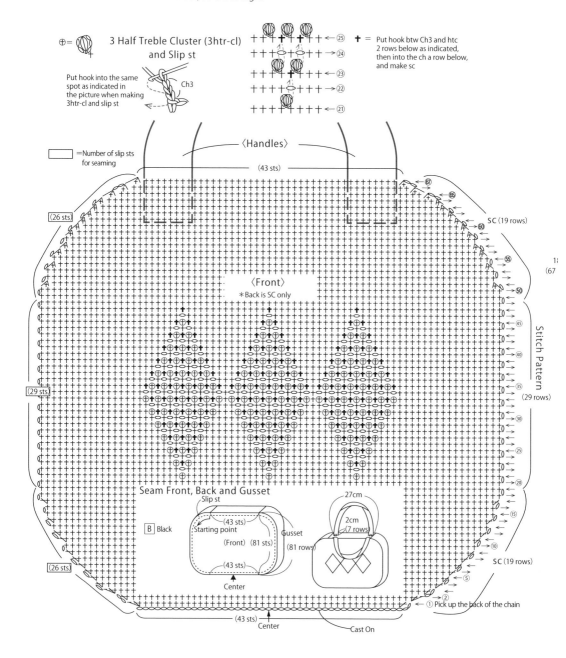

⊕ = 3 Half Treble Cluster (3htr-cl) and Slip st

Put hook into the same spot as indicated in the picture when making 3htr-cl and slip st

Ch3

✝ = Put hook btw Ch3 and htc 2 rows below as indicated, then into the ch a row below, and make sc

□ = Number of slip sts for seaming

⟨Handles⟩

(43 sts)

(26 sts)

SC (19 rows)

⟨Front⟩
*Back is SC only

Stitch Pattern

(29 sts)

(29 rows)

Seam Front, Back and Gusset

Slip st

B Black

Starting point

(43 sts)

(Front)

Gusset

(81 sts)

(81 rows)

27cm

2cm (7 rows)

(43 sts)

Center

(26 sts)

SC (19 rows)

① Pick up the back of the chain

(43 sts)
Center

Cast On

Instructions

Note: (A) uses Olive only, (B) uses MC and CC

① Front and Back - Cast On with chain st. Row 1, crochet into the back of the chain. Back is worked in sc only, Front is worked as indicated in the large chart.

② Gusset - Cast On with chain st, and start from the bottom center. Work 102 rows in sc, end with slip st on the last row. Work the other side of the Gusset by picking up the remaining two strands of the chain sts.

③ Seam Front, Back and Gusset with slip sts. (For (B), use Black yarn)

④ Make two handels, and sew them on the WS of Front and Back with whip st.

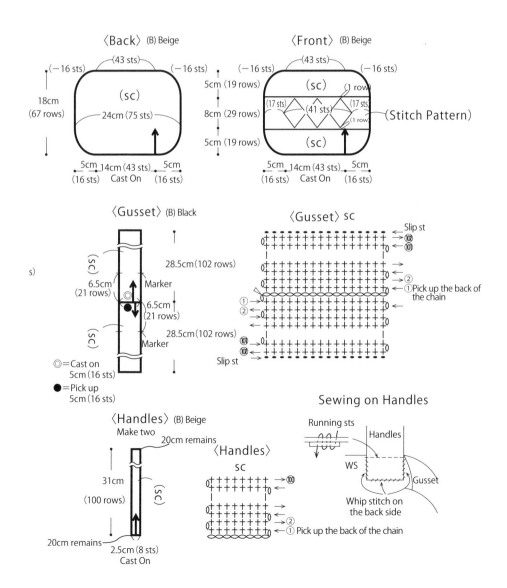

111

◆使用糸◆ダルマレース糸♯20　　オリーブ（11）…100 g（2玉）
　　　　　　　　　　　　　　ベージュ（3）…75 g（2玉）、黒（15）…25 g（1玉）

◆使用針◆2/0号かぎ針

◆ゲージ◆細編み 10cm角 31目×37段

◆できあがり寸法◆幅24cm、深さ18cm

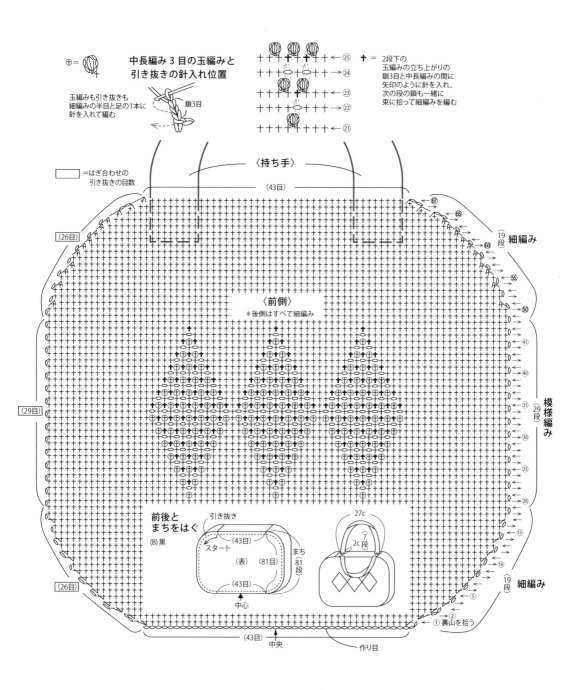

⊕= 中長編み 3 目の玉編みと
引き抜きの針入れ位置

玉編みも引き抜きも
細編みの半目と足の1本に
針を入れて編む

鎖3目

+ = 2段下の
玉編みの立ち上がりの
鎖3目と中長編みの間に
矢印のように針を入れ、
次の段の鎖も一緒に
束に拾って細編みを編む

□=はぎ合わせの
引き抜きの目数

〈持ち手〉

（43目）

〈前側〉
＊後側はすべて細編み

模様編み
（29段）

細編み
（19段）

細編み
（19段）

前後と
まちをはぐ
(B)黒

引き抜き

スタート

（43目）

（表）　（81目）

まち
（81
段）

（43目）

中心

27c

7
2c段

裏山を拾う

（43目）

中央

作り目

◆編み方要点◆ (A)はオリーブのみ、(B)は指定通り配色

①側面の前後とも鎖の作り目をし、1段めは裏山を拾って編みます。後側は細編みのみで編み、前側は途中模様編みを編みます。

②まちは、鎖の作り目をして底中心部分から編み始め、細編みを102段編み最後に引き抜きます。反対側も作り目の残りの2本を拾って同様に編みます。

③側面の前後とまちを外表に合わせて、引き抜きではぎ合わせます。続きで入れ口部分にも引き抜きます。(Bは黒を使用)

④持ち手を2本編み、前後の側面の内側にとじつけます。

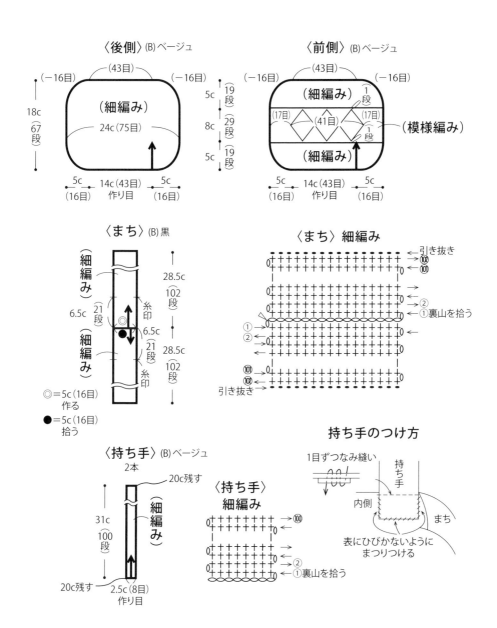

Credits

Photography	Masahiro Kohda (photos with models)
	Other photo credits are on respective pages.
Hair & Makeup	Yoko Yoshikawa
Models	Masako
Styling	Misato Sakamoto / Meri Tanaka
Editorial, Graphic Design	Meri Tanaka
Writing	Meri Tanaka, except listed on respective pages
Production Supervision	Tokuko Ochiai
Project Coord./Crt. Tech Edit	Hiromi Onishi / Tokuko Ochiai / Keiko Kikuno
Proof Reading	Beth Petrich / Keiko Kikuno / Hiromi Onishi (patterns)
	Patricia Hurley / Tokuko Ochiai (articles)
CAD Operation	Shino Uchiyama
Pattern Layout	Tokuko Ochiai / Meri Tanaka
Test Knitting	Hideko Omori / Chinatsu Okazaki / Megumi Usa
	Minako Terakawa / Junko Yanagimoto / Ririko
	Sarah Hughes / Patricia Vivacqua / Aya Yoshida
Translation	Hiromi Onishi / Keiko Kikuno / Tokuko Ochiai
	Junko Masukane (pattern)
	Meri Tanaka (articles)

Wholesale	**amirisu** is available for wholesale. For details, contact *info@amirisu.com*
Advertising	Contact *amirisu.info@gmail.com* to receive the latest rate card
Stockists	http://www.amirisu.com/wp/stockists/
Subscription	Questions regarding your subscription, info@amirisu.com
Submission	Send all submissions to *contribute@amirisu.com*
	For design submission schedule and details, subscribe to our newsletter or Facebook page.

© amirisu co. 2017 Printed in Canada by Hemlock Printers.
本書の写真、カット及び内容の無断転載を禁じます。